Barbara Marx Hubbard is an American original. In *Conscious Evolution* we see one of the great visionaries of our time make a case for why her noble vision of our future is grounded in our emerging reality.

It has become commonplace that we are going through a time of great changes, but the old order misinterprets them in belligerence, fear, and denial. Barbara Marx Hubbard offers a hopeful and clear-eyed alternative, that the meaning of changes in our time is in our call to evolutionary greatness. Her large and generous vision of the conscious evolution of humanity links our potential for a new Renaissance both to the manifestation of spirit and to evolution of our biosphere. And she shows the convergence of visionaries with leading edge science and with activists on a common view of our future. She invites us all to link up and cocreate that future.

— Paul Ray, author of
The Integral Culture Survey

With rare enthusiasm and seeping vision, Barbara Marx Hubbard presents a clear, compassionate, and practical call for humanity to awaken to our fullest potentials, both spiritual and social.

— Duane Elgin, author of
Awakening Earth and *Voluntary Simplicity*

Barbara Marx Hubbard offers a blueprint for a new, spiritually motivated "social potential movement." Based not on speculative fantasy, but on real life examples of what's working now in every sector of society. The perfect complement to Marianne Williamson's recent rallying cry for a "holistic politics" in *The Healing of America*, Hubbard's book starts where Williamson's leaves off, detailing the steps needed to actually bring about a genuine healing of our society. Read them both and cocreate the new American Renaissance.

— Eric Utne, founder,
Utne Reader

Barbara Marx Hubbard points the way for us to author our future — demonstrates that we can be the artist, the inventor of what occurs in our culture for the next several centuries. Following her direction, we can each be the creator of our collective future.

— Dave Ellis, author of
Creating Your Future

Conscious Evolution is a splendid introduction to a brilliant and engaging modern thinker. Writing in a vivid, highly personalized style, she presents her search for life's ultimate meaning and her vision of humanity's birth into the universe as a cosmic species. Hubbard focuses attention on what is perhaps the central issue of our society today: What sort of future do we want, for ourselves and the environment around us? As an intelligent species, we should want consciously to determine our future rather than just letting the future happen to us. For Hubbard, this has been a lifetime mission with numerous brilliant achievements.

— Edward Cornish, president of World Future Society

Barbara Marx Hubbard is a spiritual visionary and masterful planetary social inventor. Here she presents a grand epic poem on the coming birth of humanity...a birth forged in crisis with a deep faith in the age old process of creation. She knows people shift into higher states when the heat is turned up and makes a case for why that has always been so.

She has constructed a promise of love and hope and a system for us to get there together. It is an evolutionary path we take with nature and spirit. It is a creative rage of the heart and a blinding expression of faith that what we each do counts forever. We do with the divine and as the divine. This story must be told everywhere.

— Jim Channon, former lieutenant colonel and
founder of the First Earth Battalion in the U.S. Army

Conscious Evolution is an essential book. I recommend it enthusiastically.

— Gary Zukav, author of
The Seat of the Soul

CONSCIOUS EVOLUTION

Awakening the Power of
Our Social Potential

CONSCIOUS EVOLUTION

Awakening the Power of Our Social Potential

BARBARA MARX HUBBARD

NEW WORLD LIBRARY
NOVATO, CALIFORNIA

New World Library
14 Pamaron Way
Novato, CA 94949

© 1998 Barbara Marx Hubbard

Cover design: Big Fish
Cover photograph: Photonica
Text design & typography: Aaron Kenedi
Editorial: Becky Benenate

Library in Congress Cataloging-in-Publication Data

Hubbard, Barbara Marx, 1929 -
Conscious evolution : awakening the power of our social potential /
Barbara Marx Hubbard.
p. cm.
Includes bibliographical references.
ISBN 1-57731-016-0 (alk. paper)
1. Social evolution. 2. Social ethics. 3. Social ecology.
4. Social participation. I. Title.
HM106.H83 1997   97-14934
303.4 - dc21   CIP

First printing, January 1998
ISBN 1-57731-016-0
Printed in Canada on acid-free paper
Distributed to the trade by Publishers Group West

10 9 8 7 6 5 4

CONTENTS

PART III
THE SOCIAL POTENTIAL MOVEMENT

PART IV
THE GREAT AWAKENING

PART V
A CALL TO ACTION

ACKNOWLEDGMENTS

I wish to give my heartfelt thanks to Nancy Carroll, executive director of The Foundation for Conscious Evolution, whose loving support, tireless work, and faith have helped bring this work to fruition, and now sets the stage for its further manifestation in the world.

I am deeply grateful for my publisher, Marc Allen, who recognized this work as seminal and insisted that it be published, and to Becky Benenate, my friend, editor, and constant source of strength and encouragement. Also, I wish to thank Ann Crawford, one of the editors of *Conscious Evolution* in its earliest form.

Avon Mattison has been of inestimable loving help.

My deep appreciation goes to Prof. A. Harris Stone for his stimulating interest and editorial help in developing these ideas, his instigation of "Socratic Dialogues" to lay the foundations of this book, and his pioneering efforts to bring conscious evolution as a new field into the academic world.

My special appreciation goes to Hazel Henderson, one of the great social innovators of our time who has encouraged me with her loving friendship for 20 years.

I deeply acknowledge Bill Gray, whose life is dedicated to bringing human potential in all its forms onto television, and who has guided and cared for me and these ideas with skill and devotion.

I want to thank Neale Donald Walsch, author of *Conversations with God: An Uncommon Dialogue* for his understanding and brilliant ability to communicate widely and broadly to masses of people about this work.

My heartfelt thanks goes to my beloved patron Laurance S. Rockefeller who has supported this work with fidelity, inspiration and generosity.

My loving thanks goes to Sidney Lanier, who has carried the seed idea of conscious evolution in his heart, and nourishes it in me. And to Earl Hubbard with whom so many of these ideas were conceived.

In a special category, I wish to acknowledge the extraordinary input of my friend and colleague Mark Donohue. He spent hundreds of hours with me helping to bring the vision into greater clarity and pragmatic usefulness. His assistance was of incomparable value. As a young, socially responsible business man he understands how to apply this vast new world conscious evolution to the pratical purpose of evolving capitalism itself. He can be an important communicator and developer of this work in the world.

FOREWORD

BY NEALE DONALD WALSCH

By now, few people can seriously doubt that we are moving through one of the most crucial and important periods in human history. The past twenty-five years have placed sufficient evidence before all of us. Political upheavals alone have overthrown (and that is an apt word) our longest-lived conventions and constructions. Add the social, economic, scientific, educational, and spiritual reorderings we are witnessing and we have the recipe for much larger revolutions.

What makes this particular period so revolutionary is that people are now *doing* rather than simply watching all of this. They are taking hold of the apple cart and shaking the hell out of it. And that is exactly what they are trying to do: shake the hell right out of it.

This is a shakedown cruise. What we do and how we do it over the next few years will set the course for Spaceship Earth (as Buckminster Fuller so eloquently described it) for the next century and well beyond — if, indeed, the ship is allowed to survive at all. And it is her survival we are talking about here. I think most people now understand that.

I believe the human race is beginning to lose patience with itself, and with the way it has threatened its own existence. Those threats are still all around us, of course. But at least we now see them and realize that *we* have built them into our politics, our economics, our theologies, our social and educational systems. We are now ready to admit that our very way of doing things on this planet led us to this critical juncture, and so we are dismantling much of what we have put in place. This has produced some consternation among those who have become attached to the "old ways."

Not all of that concern is misplaced.

Our collective shift, our movement, from observer, to unwitting participant, to conscious, cocreative cause in the recreation of our combined experience is what renders this time in our race's history so pregnant with possibilities — and dangers.

To what are we going to give birth? The paradise, at last, of which we have all so long dreamed, or the self-inflicted damnations of our worst nightmares? Will we be successful in getting the hell out of our lives, or will we bring more of it in, until we finally destroy our planet altogether with one final foolishness?

Much will depend on how we respond to the challenges and invitations of this remarkable time, described and clarified in this sweeping book of breathtaking scope by Barbara Marx Hubbard. An urgent call from one of the most extraordinary visionaries of our time, *Conscious Evolution: Awakening the Power of Our Social Potential* is a document of stunning insight, including a blueprint for the recreation of human reality so brilliantly and originally conceived, and so obviously and completely right, that it cannot help but propel the most ambitious among us to a new level of commitment to, and excited cocreation of, our future.

That is what is required now: Ambition. We must get off our collective duffs and arouse in ourselves a deep desire to produce our future, rather than wait to see what future is produced.

We have been asleep, and it is time for us to wake up.

Barbara Marx Hubbard — this incredible futurist, this breathtaking social seer — is the songbird of our new morning. This book is her melody. It is a tune to make the human heart sing, to make the soul dance again.

It is beautiful music to wake up to.

— Neale Donald Walsch
Author of *Conversations with God, Book I* and *II*
Ashland, Oregon

"We are at the very point in time when a 400-year old age is dying and another is struggling to be born — a shifting of culture, science, society, and institutions enormously greater than the world has ever experienced. Ahead, the possibility of the regeneration of individuality, liberty, community, and ethics such as the world has never known, and a harmony with nature, with one another, and with the divine intelligence such as the world has never dreamed."

— Dee Ward Hock
founder of Visa

CONSCIOUS EVOLUTION

**Awakening the Power of
Our Social Potential**

INTRODUCTION

onscious Evolution: Awakening the Power of Our Social Potential is an early effort to respond to the immense challenge and opportunity of our age. It sets forth a vision of the vast transformational enterprise of the next millennium, and it seeks to discover the design of evolution inherent in all nature with which we can consciously cooperate to guide our actions. It is a design of how a planet makes its transition from its high-technology, polluting, and overpopulating phase to a system that fulfills its collective potential. It reveals a spirit-motivated plan of action based on the patterns of evolutionary success and suggests how we can ease the transition by identifying key ideas, processes, people, and activities now fulfilling elements of this design.

Conscious Evolution carries us beyond the human potential movement toward the social potential movement and describes a new social architecture to enhance and connect social innovations now evolving our world. *Conscious Evolution* identifies, out of the breakdowns in modern society, systemic breakthroughs demonstrating that we are in the midst of a positive quantum change — a metamorphosis of humanity.

Conscious Evolution presents a plan that can bring humanity across the dangerous threshold of possible self-destruction to the point of the shift — when we realize we are going to make it, that we have the capacity to survive and grow. This plan is composed of initiatives that are already occurring, but have not yet been connected, communicated, and understood to be vital elements of a whole system transition.

The plan has five elements (comprising the five parts of this book). Each element is vital to the design of our transition.

The first element relates to the new story of creation. It is essential we understand that the universe has a history. Evolution's astonishing capacity for novelty, emergence, and transformation that has brought us from subatomic particles to our current condition is still at work. Simply stated, the nature of nature is to transform.

Through awareness of the recurring patterns in the process of evolution, we gain a new view of ourselves as active participants in the creation — cocreators with the process of evolution. The whole evolutionary journey is seen as the story of the birth of a universal humanity. Our current crises are understood as the crises of the birth of the next stage of our evolution, dangerous but natural.

The second element requires us to understand and develop the new worldview called conscious evolution. Conscious evolution is presented as an emerging idea of the nature of reality that can guide us in the ethical and creative use of our power toward the next stage of human evolution.

The third element awakens our social potential. A new social architecture is presented whereby we can accelerate the connections among innovating people and projects to shift humanity toward a more positive future. Media and education to foster conscious evolution are presented.

The fourth element heralds the great awakening. A world-changing event is described as a way to align our higher consciousnesses with our emerging capacities. It is designed to create a global mind change and launch us into the Third Millennium with hope in our hearts. A vision of a cocreative society, what it may be like if everything works, is offered.

The fifth element invites you to participate by finding and fulfilling your life purpose through organizations, activities, and teams already moving toward conscious evolution.

Conscious Evolution is written specifically for those who have recognized the desire to transform and grow. It is a call to each generation to fulfill its creative potential. It provides tools and opportunities for each of us to participate in the greatest adventure in human history.

This is our finest hour. We live in a unique time, perhaps as significant as when the first humans arose in self-consciousness in an animal world. Millions of us are rising in a more universal, holistic, or cosmic consciousness in a self-centered world. We are being called forth in every field and discipline to fulfill our potential through joining together in creative action. In the Gospel According to Thomas it is said, "If you bring forth what is within you, what you bring forth will save you. If you do not bring forth what is within you, what you do not bring forth will destroy you."

As we participate in this grand adventure, we will bring forth all that is within us and not only save ourselves, but evolve our world.

For me this book is the culmination of 30 years as a futurist, lecturer, author, and spiritual and social explorer. In Thomas's words, it is a way of bringing forth what is in me, and I hope it will help to call forth what is within you.

My quest has been to understand and encourage our collective potential to evolve. All my adult life I have been exploring with colleagues throughout the world how we can have a graceful, peaceful, and gentle birth rather than further violence and suffering that has been foreseen. *Conscious Evolution* is the fruit of this search.

I hope to continue serving as a catalyst for the social potential movement, in dialogue with people in every sector of society as to how we can best apply the ideas of conscious evolution to our challenges and opportunities in health, education, environment, government, business, spiritual growth, and the arts and sciences. Equally important, I seek to embody the qualities of a cocreative human — to combine the human and social potential movements in myself.

I do believe that within the next 10 years we can discover and commit to an evolutionary agenda. I believe we will have had a global awakening and will begin consciously and ethically to use our vast collective powers for the evolution of our species. It is to this vision of our collective emergence that *Conscious Evolution* is dedicated.

PART I

THE NEW STORY OF CREATION

CHAPTER ONE

The Awakening of Humanity

Occasionally, in the course of history a new worldview emerges that transforms society. It happened when Jesus' disciples were inspired by his life to believe in radical transformation through love. It occurred in the Renaissance when the idea of progress through knowledge was born. It happened in the United States when the ideas of freedom and democracy became institutions through the Constitution and the Bill of Rights, and again among the transcendentalists, such as Ralph Waldo Emerson and Walt Whitman, who believed that each individual is an expression of the divine, a free and sovereign person. Now, once again a new worldview is arising. This idea is the culmination of all human history. It holds the promise of fulfilling the great aspirations of the past and heralds the advent of the next phase of our evolution. It is the idea of *conscious evolution.*

Conscious evolution is occurring in our generation because we are now gaining an understanding of the processes of nature: the gene, the atom, the brain, the origin of the universe, and the whole story of creation from the big bang to us. We are now changing our understanding of how nature evolves; we are moving from unconscious evolution through natural selection to conscious evolution by choice. With this increased knowledge and the power that it gives us, we can destroy the world or we can participate in a future of immeasurable dimensions. Into our hands has been given the power of codestruction or cocreation.

As Jonas Salk stated in *Anatomy of Reality*,

> The most meaningful activity in which a human being can be engaged is one that is directly related to human evolution. This is true because human beings now play an active and critical role not only in the process of their own evolution but in the survival and evolution of all living beings. Awareness of this places upon human beings a responsibility for their participation in and contribution to the process of evolution. If humankind would accept and acknowledge this responsibility and become creatively engaged in the process of metabiological evolution consciously, as well as unconsciously, a new reality would emerge, and a new age would be born.[1]

Consciousness has evolved for billions of years, from single cells to animals to humans, but *conscious* evolution is radically new. In *The Life Era*, Prof. Eric Chaisson, of the Wright Center for Scientific Education, suggested that the second great event in the history of the universe is happening now.[2] The first event was when matter gained charge of radiative energy, which organized the explosive energy of supernovas into metals and materials that formed the material world more than 10 billion years ago. The second is when technologically competent human life gains an understanding of matter. As we learn how nature's invisible processes work, we can restore the environment of our Earth and free ourselves from poverty and disease; we can design new life forms, bring life to other planets, and eventually explore and bring Earth life into the universe. Eric Chaisson wrote in *ZYGON,*

> The change from matter-dominance to life-dominance is the second of two preeminent events in the history of the universe.... If our species is to survive and enjoy a future, then we must make synonymous the words future and ethical, thus terming our next grand evolutionary epoch, ethical evolution.[3]

Evolution or Extinction

An irreversible shift toward conscious evolution began in 1945 when the United States dropped atomic bombs on Hiroshima and Nagasaki. With this dreadful release of power we penetrated one of the invisible technologies of nature — the atom — and gained the power that we once attributed to the gods. This capability, combined with other rapidly developing technologies such as biotechnology, nanotechnology (the ability to build atom by atom), and artificial intelligence, if used in our current state of self-centered consciousness could lead to the destruction of the human race. We must learn "ethical evolution," as Chaisson said. And we do not have hundreds of years in which to learn.

The response to this crisis has been an uprising of a new consciousness — almost a new kind of humanity. From the 1960s to the 1990s the metamorphosis accelerated as millions of people became aware of environmental degradation, social injustice, and the need for radical change. We entered a period of confusion — a loss of vision and direction. We continued to destroy our rain forests, pollute our soil and water, and increase our rate of population growth.

(Our global population is now approaching 6 billion people. Another doubling of the population — expected to happen within the next 40 years — will bring us beyond the estimated carrying capacity of Earth.) If we continue with our current practices, we are likely to destroy ourselves. Many of us have seen looming catastrophe, but few of us have realized that this crisis is driving us toward positive change, toward a quantum transformation.

Imaginal Cells

Let's compare our situation with the metamorphosis of a caterpillar into a butterfly. When the caterpillar weaves its cocoon, imaginal disks begin to appear. These disks embody the blueprint of the butterfly yet to come. Although the disks are a natural part of the caterpillar's evolution, its immune system recognizes them as foreign and tries to destroy them. As the disks arrive faster and begin to link up, the caterpillar's immune system breaks down and its body begins to disintegrate. When the disks mature and become imaginal cells, they form themselves into a new pattern, thus transforming the disintegrating body of the caterpillar into the butterfly. The breakdown of the caterpillar's old system is essential for the breakthrough of the new butterfly. Yet, in reality the caterpillar neither dies nor disintegrates, for from the beginning its hidden purpose was to transform and be reborn as the butterfly.

By applying this analogy, we can see that during the 1960s our social systems started to become dysfunctional, or began to "disintegrate," as we experienced the cold war and the threat to the environment, the growing population crisis, pollution, and social inequities. As people started waking up, they became imaginal disks in the body of society. The environmental movement, the antiwar movement, the Apollo space program, the women's movement, the civil rights and human rights movements, new music, transcendental meditation, yoga, and mind-expanding substances all encouraged a young generation to act as instruments of social transformation — striving to birth the still-invisible societal butterfly. But if we had been offered the opportunity to form a new kind of society, we would have collapsed. We were too young, too few, and too inexperienced to bring forth a more just, humane, and life-enhancing society at that time. And often when new leaders did step forward, they were attacked by society's immune system fighting to maintain the old social order of the caterpillar: witness the assassinations of Gandhi, John F. Kennedy, and Martin Luther King, Jr.

The new social processes, structures, and systems to create better education, universal health care, economic justice, regenerative development, and many other requirements of the coming age had not yet emerged — and are still barely formed. Although we began to develop ourselves as individuals in the spiritual and human potential movement, there was as yet no coherent social potential movement to guide us in the evolution of our communities and of society as a whole.

During the past 30 years, our basic social and economic systems have attempted to maintain the status quo despite the many warnings that the old ways, particularly in the developed world, were no longer sustainable. In many instances our existing systems are not humane; homelessness, hunger, disease, and poverty consume the lives of hundreds of millions of people and the environment continues to degrade. We can view the reactive and conservative ways of the past few decades as a survival mechanism — as the caterpillar's immune system rigidly holding on to old structures until new social systems are mature enough to function. As we enter the 21st century, millions of people are awakening in every field, culture, and ethnic group. The imaginal disks are linking up, are becoming imaginal cells, and are beginning to proliferate throughout the social body. Each person who says "I know I can be more," "I can do more," "The world does not have to be this way" is an imaginal cell in the emerging culture of humanity. The social immune system is beginning to surrender as the new consciousness arises everywhere.

In *Global Consciousness Change: Indicators of an Emerging Paradigm*, Duane Elgin with Coleen LeDrew wrote,

> From this inquiry, we have concluded that a new global culture and consciousness have taken root and are beginning to grow in the world. This represents a shift in consciousness as distinct and momentous as that which occurred in the transition from the agricultural era to the industrial era roughly three hundred years ago.... This change in consciousness has two primary features. First, there is a further awakening of our unique capacity to be self-reflective — to stand back from the rush of life and, with greater detachment, observe the world and its workings non-judgmentally. Second, from this more spacious perspective, the Earth (and even the cosmos) are seen as interconnected, living systems.[4]

Cultural Creatives

It seems as though imaginal cells are beginning to gain ascendancy. This phenomenon is vividly presented in *The Integral Culture Survey: A Study of Transformational Values in America.*[5] Noted social analyst Paul H. Ray revealed through extensive research that there are 44 million "cultural creatives" in the United States alone — almost one-fourth the American population. Cultural creatives are defined by a set of values, a new lifestyle, and worldview. Feeling that we are all members of one planet, they are concerned about the environment and social-economic justice. They have a different notion of relationship — one that is less hierarchical. They are interested in holistic health and are extending women's concerns into the public domain. Their emphasis is on consciousness raising in all aspects of our lives — personal, social, and planetary.

Cultural creatives are social idealists, concerned not so much with political and economic power as those in the old movement were, but rather with seeking to change our image of the world, our sense of identity. Cultural creatives originated in the great social movements of the 1960s and are now maturing, taking their stand for a more spiritualized, personalized, and integrated culture.

According to Ray, cultural creatives are the fastest growing subculture in the United States, yet most of these creative individuals feel they are alone. They have not yet sensed their connection with one another or with the pattern and momentum of the collective change they represent. Nonetheless, as Marilyn Ferguson wrote in her seminal work *The Aquarian Conspiracy*,

> A leaderless but powerful network is working to bring about radical change in the United States. Its members have broken with certain key elements of Western thought, and they may even have broken continuity with history.[6]

These are the imaginal cells of the social body.

This emerging social potential movement is not revolutionary, but evolutionary. Its aim is not to destroy, but to fulfill. When the butterfly emerges, it doesn't deny the caterpillar — it is the caterpillar evolved. This movement is not an attack on another group or an assertion that "our way is better." The movement is not here to *attack* but to *attract*. Its purpose is to evolve all of us, our communities, and our world so that all people are free to fulfill their highest potential.

Today, cultural creatives are communicating ever more rapidly with one another (especially through the Internet), affirming and reinforcing the new emerging pattern. Thousands of transformational workshops, trainings, and teachings are appearing in mainstream businesses, churches, and organizations. Books by new paradigm teachers and leaders consistently reach the bestseller lists. Through resonance, or echoing and reinforcing one another, values of inclusivity, spirituality, attunement with other species, and ecological sensitivity are spreading. These values are not new; many are ancient, yet they are emerging now in a new way that is vital to the survival of the whole system.

This book is a call to those who are experiencing a deep motivation to be more, to find their life purpose and to contribute their gifts to the evolution of the world. There are countless such individuals who have been maturing over the past 30 years, yet they are infrequently at the heads of corporations, governments, or traditional religions because their current function is to evolve and expand systems, not to maintain the current power structure as it is.

Although the desire for something more is widespread, often that something is not known. We lack a vision of what we want to create. Inquiries, conferences, and symposia throughout the world seek answers to major problems, yet something is still missing — we don't see where we are going; we have few positive visions of our next stage of evolution.

Our media, which is like a planetary nervous system, are far more sensitive to breakdowns than to breakthroughs. They filter out our creativity and successes, considering them less newsworthy than violence, war, and dissent. When we read newspapers and watch television news, we feel closer to a death in the social body than to an awakening. Yes, something is dying; however, the media do not recognize that something is also being born.

The Noosphere

A radically new phenomenon has emerged worldwide, but it has not yet been recognized. It is called the "noosphere" by Teilhard de Chardin, in his famous work *The Phenomenon of Man.*[7] The root of the word is *noos*, meaning mind. The noosphere is the mind-sphere, the thinking layer of Earth, the larger social body created by human intelligence. It is composed of all the spiritual, cultural, social, and technological capacities of humanity, seen as one interrelated superorganism. It is formed from our languages, our art and music, our religious and social structures, our constitutions, our communication systems, our microscopes, our telescopes, our cars, planes, rockets, laboratories, and more. Although we inherited the geosphere, the hydrosphere, and the biosphere, we have generated the noosphere.

We as individuals have not changed much physiologically or intellectually in the last 2,000 years, but our larger social body — the noosphere — has become radically empowered. We are now being born into an extended social and scientific capacity that has never before existed on Earth. It is through this collective social body of shared intelligence, capacities, and systems that we go to the moon, map our genes, clone a sheep, and transmit our television images around the world at the speed of light. It is with this body that we codestroy or cocreate. It is into this body that we imaginal cells are born — the still-invisible societal butterfly. Conscious evolution has arisen at this precise moment of history because the noosphere has matured and has given humanity powers to affect evolution by choice.

We cannot see the noosphere. Neither our past philosophies or religions nor our social, economic, technological, or scientific systems have yet been able to encompass or guide the power of this collective body — a body that has been built by human endeavor and intelligence. With the advent of the idea of ethical and conscious evolution, however, we may be able to discover the path of action that will lead us toward an immeasurable and positive future.

Without such a new and guiding worldview, further development of the planetary system will be increasingly distorted and destructive. If, however, we can see the glory of the noosphere maturing toward an immeasurable future for the human race — a future that attracts us, and calls forth our gifts — we will then serve the purpose of awakening the whole body to its capacity.

The Social Potential Movement

The human potential movement began more than 30 years ago with the seminal work of Abraham H. Maslow, Victor Frankl, Robert Assogioli, and others who discovered, nurtured, and affirmed the higher reaches of human nature. They developed techniques and practices to fulfill untapped human potential. In his seminal book, *Toward a Psychology of Being*, Maslow identified a hierarchy of human needs inherent in all of us. He said that we all have basic needs for survival, security, and self-esteem. When these basic needs are relatively well met, a new set of needs arises naturally. They are growth needs for self-expression in work that is intrinsically valuable and self-rewarding. Then, transcendent needs emerge: to be connected to the larger whole — one with Source — to transcend the limits of self-centered consciousness itself.[8]

Maslow had the genius to study "well" people rather than the sick and discovered that all fully functioning, joyful, productive, and self-actualizing people have one trait in common: chosen work or vocation. If we do not find life purpose at the growth stage, he reasoned, we become sick, depressed, even violent. People in modern society, he said, are stuck between survival needs and growth needs for further self-expression and self-actualization in a culture of intrinsic meaning.

Through the human potential movement millions of us have awakened, crossing the barrier from survival to growth needs. Yet, ultimately all of us want to find life purpose and meaning — a potentially huge community of people, perhaps a majority in the developed world (where basic needs are relatively well met).

The social potential movement builds on the human potential movement. It identifies peaks of social creativity and works toward social wellness the same way the human potential movement culti- vates personal wellness. It seeks out social innovations and designs social systems that work toward a life-enhancing global society. I believe the social potential movement is on the threshold of a mass awakening, seeking to carry into society what individuals have learned spiritually and personally.

An Evolutionary Agenda

The social potential movement is the vital catalyst to carry us into the 21st century and to fulfill our collective potential in the Third Millennium. It is now surfacing in society and is ready for a collec- tive vision that attracts and connects us, not only with one another but with society as a whole. The time is ripe to move toward a new *evolutionary* agenda — not to reform but to transform based on the full and appropriate use of our immense new powers. This agenda is based on the hierarchy of social needs, which calls upon us to:

- meet basic food and shelter needs of all people;
- limit our population growth;
- restore Earth's environment;

- learn to coexist with other species;
- learn sustainable economic development;
- shift the vast military-industrial-technological complex toward building new worlds on Earth and in space;
- redesign social and economic systems to enhance human compassion, cooperation, and creativity;
- emancipate individuals' unique potential and life purpose;
- explore and develop the further reaches of the human spirit and the universe beyond the planet of our birth.

What would happen if we began to use our new powers within such an evolutionary, open-ended agenda? Ancient prophesies have foreseen our self-destruction, but few of us have seen the magnificence of what we could become, collectively, through the use of all our powers — spiritual, social, and scientific. In the past our glorious visions of the future — heaven, paradise, nirvana — were thought to happen after death. The newer thought is that we do not have to die to get there! We are not speaking here of life after death in some mythical heaven, but life more abundant in real time in history. We are speaking of the next stage of our social evolution.

A Spirit-Motivated Plan of Action for the 21st Century

We now know that a plan of action or program is encoded in the genes of every living organism that guides it from conception through gestation, birth, maturation, and death. Planet Earth is a living system. Is it not possible, then, that there is a prepatterned (but not a predetermined) pattern or tendency, an encoded design for planetary evolution just as there is for biological evolution? There is a biological cycle. It is possible that there is also a planetary life cycle. Earth's conception occurred with the big bang. The period of gestation included its 15 billion years of evolution, from its formation $4^{1}/_{2}$ billion years ago to human life. Its birth is happening now as we awaken to ourselves as one planetary body, capable of destroying ourselves or cocreating an immeasurable future. And we know that $4^{1}/_{2}$ billion years from now our sun will expand and destroy all the planets in the solar system. We live precisely midway in the life cycle of our planet. We have not yet seen another planet go through this change, so we have nothing with which to compare. But let us imagine for the moment that we are a normal event in the universe and that there is a pattern encoded in our collective spiritual, social, and scientific awareness, ready to be activated when the time for conscious evolution is here, just as the imaginal cells appear when the caterpillar is ready to transform.

To awaken our magnificent social potential, we need first and foremost to know our "new story." This story places us in the cosmos and reveals to us our vital part in the evolution of ourselves and our world.

I believe such a design exists for our planetary evolution, that the crises and opportunities we face today are triggering the next stage of this design, and that we, as individual members of the planetary body, are now being awakened to our new personal and social capacities to participate in our evolution. It is not a plan imposed by any group or individual, but rather a design of evolution, a tendency with which we can cooperate more consciously to repattern our social systems and evolve ourselves. The word "plan" here does not connote a fixed and predetermined path that we must follow. Rather, it means that we are seeking the inherent pattern or design in evolution that tends toward higher consciousness and greater freedom through more complex order, so that we can formulate specific and pragmatic plans of action based on that tendency.

CHAPTER TWO

Discovering the Importance of the New Story

I t was a cold November day in Paris in 1948 during my junior year abroad from Bryn Mawr College. Somehow I had separated myself from my classmates and wandered into Chez Rosalie, a small café on the Left Bank. A wood fire was burning and the smell of Gauloises cigarettes filled the air.

I sat at one of the wooden tables and ordered my lunch. A tall, handsome young man opened the door, letting in the cold. There was only one place left for him to sit, opposite me. I smiled at him. He had such a special intensity that I decided to ask him questions that had dominated my thoughts ever since the United States dropped the atomic bombs on Japan three years earlier: What is the meaning of our new technological powers? What is the purpose of Western civilization? What is a positive image of the future commensurate with these new powers?

In my quest for answers, I had read through philosophy, science fiction, and world religions. But amazingly, except for brief glimpses in science fiction and mystical revelation, I found none. The philosophers looked back toward a golden age, as the Greeks did; or were cyclical, as in Eastern thought; or were stoical, believing there was "nothing new under the sun" as the Roman philosopher Marcus Aurelius said; or were existentialist, like Jean Paul Sartre and Albert Camus, proclaiming that the universe has no inherent meaning except what we give it as individuals. Finally, I read the materialistic philosophers who proclaimed that the universe is nothing but matter and is inevitably degenerating to a "heat death" through increasing disorder or entropy as stars burn out, and with them all life will die. Although some visionaries and mystics foresaw a life beyond this life, beyond death, I found no positive visions of the future to work toward in *this* life.

With these questions I became a metaphysical seeker. My upbringing had been Jewish agnostic. I was a spiritual tabula rasa — a blank slate with no religious beliefs. When I asked my father "What religion are we?" he answered, "You are an American. Do your best!" But at what? I wondered. My father was a Horatio Alger type, a poor boy from Brooklyn who had become the toy king of the world. He told his children that the purpose of life was to win, to make money. But I couldn't believe him. I knew that even if everyone had money, everyone would be as frustrated as I was, seeking the meaning of life but finding nothing. Material comfort alone could not be the goal of existence.

If I did not know life's larger purpose, how could I know my own purpose? I felt an intense need for meaning and was obsessed with these questions, reading through world literature on a passionate quest to find an answer. I had asked my questions of every young man I dated. What is the purpose of our new powers? And what is your purpose? They had no idea! I never received a good answer — until that day in Paris.

We talked casually for a few moments, then I asked the young man my questions. He looked at me with gray-green eyes, took a long drag on his Gauloises, and said, "I am an artist. My purpose is to seek a new image of humanity commensurate with our new power to shape the future."

I'm going to marry you! flashed through my mind . . . and I did.

As we sat at the little table that afternoon, he explained that when a culture has a story everyone understands, it gives direction and meaning to that culture. When people no longer believe the story, the culture disintegrates.

For example, when the Homeric legends — the stories of the gods and goddesses, the heroes, the Trojan War — were written, 5th-century Greece was born. As time went on, the legends no longer seemed believable and a new story emerged. That story was the Gospels, which told of one man whose life and promise changed the world. We may never know the accurate history of Jesus' life, but we do know that the story created an expectation in the human heart that brought forth a new culture, one in which the individual is sacred, the kingdom of heaven is within us, and eternal life is promised through love of God and one another. Christendom was born, and in a variety of forms it dominated the Western world for more than a thousand years. But gradually, with the advent of science and democracy some 300 years ago, the literal interpretation of the Gospels was no longer possible for millions of people.

In the Renaissance a new story emerged. It was the story of progress through knowledge, through awareness of how nature works, and through the liberation of individual freedom. In 1486 Giovanni Pico della Mirandola wrote in *Oration on the Dignity of Man*, "We have made you a creature of neither heaven nor Earth, neither mortal nor immortal, in order that you may as the free and proud shaper of your own being, fashion yourself in any form you prefer."[1]

From the Renaissance until the 20th century the story of human freedom and progress has carried us forward, but instead of inevitable advancement we are now heading toward possible global catastrophe: the breakdown of our environment, overpopulation, social alienation, dire poverty — a future worse than the past. The 20th century is the most violent and cruel in the history of humanity, with the destruction of millions of innocent people in wars and genocides. The story of hope that created the modern age is fading rapidly. More of the same will destroy us.

Now we are between stories. We are wielding massive powers; we are overconsuming and overdefending while children starve and the environment deteriorates.

In the midst of our confusion, however, a new story of evolution is emerging that has the potential to inspire us to creative action. It is coming from the combined insights of many disciplines: scientific, historical, psychological, ecological, social, spiritual, and futuristic. But it has not yet found its artistic or popular expression. We discover fragments in journals, poems, books, lectures, conferences, seminars, and networks of those interested in it. We see flashes in science fiction films. But it has not yet been pieced together and told with the power required to awaken the social potential within us and to guide us in the 21st century toward a future of infinite possibilities.

Understanding the new story is the first critical action necessary to carry us — without greater violence and suffering — toward a future equal to our full potential. Understanding will give us a sense of direction, hope, and meaning, providing us with a new self-image and positive visions of a future we choose and toward which our new powers can be used.

CHAPTER THREE

The Evolutionary Spiral

To understand our new story, we must look at our past as a movie of creation, a photogenesis, accelerated in time. It can best be visualized as an evolutionary spiral unfolding as one continuous process of transformation, from the origin of the physical universe — the big bang — through the formation of Earth, single-celled life, multicellular life, early human life, and now to us, going around the next turn of the spiral, as described in *The Evolutionary Journey*.[1]

This story is not outside ourselves. It is within, as much as the process of our growth from a fertilized egg to a newborn infant is inherent in us. We are coded not only with the memory of our personal prenatal history, but also with our cosmic history. In *The Adventure of Self-Discovery*, psychologist Stanislov Grof asserted that consciousness "has the potential to reach all aspects of existence. This includes biological birth, embryonic and fetal development, the moment of conception, as well as ancestral, racial, karmic, and phylogentic history."[2]

The experience of generations of existence lies in our genes. We are the product of 15 billion years of unbroken "success," the off-spring of untold generations of procreative victories. We originated from the first cell and can cherish as our inheritance the efforts of ancestral organisms struggling through the sea and the air, over the land and the rocks, and in the trees — all of whom survived to reproduce.

We hold the mystery of this unbroken chain of life within our body-minds. Our blood and bones were formed from the material of Earth, which, in turn, was born of stardust. In our cells is the memory of the first life. In our brains are reptilian, mammalian, and early human experiences, as so beautifully described in Daniel C. Matt's *God and the Big Bang.*[3]

We are the universe in person. Our exquisite eyes originated in the first glimmer of light sensitivity in early cells. When we wake with fear in the middle of the night, our hair standing on the backs of our necks, our nervous systems are remembering the fear of unprotected animals. When we experience our own desire for trans-formation, we are feeling the universe evolving through us.

We can witness the new story of creation as the conception, gestation, and birth of a universal humanity capable of understanding the processes of creation and cocreating with them.

The New Story of Creation

Universe The new story begins in the Great Emptiness, the void, the field of all possibilities — the mind of God. Approximately 15 billion years ago, out of *no thing* at all, in one quantum instant appeared everything that potentially is. The spark of life that animates each of us was lit at the dawn of creation. In those first 3 seconds after the original "flaring forth," as cosmologist Brian

Swimme called it in *The Universe Story*, the precise design was established that led to matter, life, self-reflective consciousness, and, now, our awakening to the whole process of creation.[4]

THE 15 BILLION-YEAR STORY OF OUR BIRTH

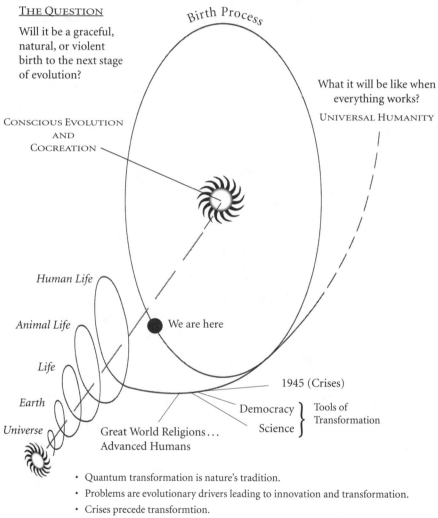

THE QUESTION

Will it be a graceful, natural, or violent birth to the next stage of evolution?

Birth Process

What it will be like when everything works?

UNIVERSAL HUMANITY

CONSCIOUS EVOLUTION
AND
COCREATION

Human Life

Animal Life

We are here

Life

1945 (Crises)

Earth

Democracy ⎫ Tools of
            ⎬ Transformation
Science   ⎭

Universe

Great World Religions...
Advanced Humans

- Quantum transformation is nature's tradition.
- Problems are evolutionary drivers leading to innovation and transformation.
- Crises precede transformtion.
- Holism is inherent in the nature of reality.
- Evolution raises consciousness and freedom through more complex order.

Earth

Our solar system and Earth was formed 4 ¹/₂ billion years ago. Radiative energy condensed and became the metals and materials of our Earth.

Life

Then, 3 ¹/₂ billion years ago single-celled life appeared in Earth's seas. Sentient consciousness emerged. Life became semi-immortal — it divided to reproduce. For billions of years the seas filled with life, absorbing the nutrients of Earth.

At some point single-celled life hit a growth limit and began overpopulating, polluting, and stagnating. Faced with this threat, life might have attempted to adapt to limitations, but instead it innovated and transformed. The problem then became an evolutionary driver.

Multicellular Life

Oxygen appeared, a poison to anaerobic cells. In an extraordinarily complex process, a new form of organism evolved: multicellular life that could metabolize oxygen. With multicellular life a jump in consciousness occurred: animal, or present-oriented consciousness, emerged in the world of single cells. Evolutionary innovations of great significance appeared, such as sexual reproduction. Instead of dividing to reproduce, multicellular organisms learned to join their genes to create new life. The rudimentary beginnings of love were born. The joining of genes produced newness, diversity — the origin of the species. Yet, a more somber revolution occurred with sexuality. Death entered the scene. Cells learned to degenerate and die. The offspring lived to reproduce anew. But sex and death are not eternal verities; they are evolutionary innovations of tremendous value. They appeared together in the process of evolution. And as we shall see, in our lifetime they are evolving together into a new form.

Hundreds of millions of years ago the first industrial revolution occurred, as space scientist Krafft Ehricke called it.[5] Through the process of photosynthesis, the barren planet was colonized and the verdant biosphere emerged. Every nook and cranny filled with life. Out of the crises on early Earth, the next stage of evolution emerged.

Human Life   Several million years ago humanity appeared — the next turn on the spiral. Imagine awakening in the animal world with the first flickering of human awareness. Self-consciousness must have been unstable then, just as cosmic consciousness flickers on and off in us now. We must have sensed that we were different and felt separate and afraid. We became future oriented, foresaw our own death, and sought to overcome it. Death's ancient clock, set millions of years earlier at the dawn of multicellular life, was challenged by the human spirit, which sought to go beyond humanoid limits. We looked upward toward the stars and yearned for more, for a life beyond this life. We buried food with our dead. We had intimations of immortality. We listened for voices and heard signals from gods, from higher beings. The universe appeared alive.

Yet we were born into a natural system of killing and being killed. Earth is an environment of violence. Millions of species act as biological weapons, consuming each other alive for survival. For all our cruel behavior, however, humans were the first to attempt not to kill, to try to preserve species, to bring compassion into the natural system. We inherited the natural trait of carnivorous behavior, yet eventually felt guilty about killing.

Then an evolutionary flame of expectation ignited. The monumental struggle to overcome primitive conditions began. Through tools, language, religion, art, and agriculture we strove for something new, something more. Goddess-worshipping cultures and native peoples established a relatively peaceful, creative balance with nature based on the equality of female and male, as described by Riane Eisler in *The Chalice and the Blade*.[6]

Recently, about 5,000 years ago, a glimmering of the next turn on the spiral arose with the great mystics who founded the religions of the world. They were future humans, foreshadowing what is to come next through us. They began to attune to a higher reality, a spiritual impulse. The universal intelligence animating every atom, molecule, and cell broke through into human consciousness. Cosmic consciousness flickered in a self-conscious world.

Each culture on Earth is patterned at the core with the inspiration given by those advanced humans. Although there was a tragic shift away from more peaceful prehistoric societies, those patriarchal religions set the ground for a quantum jump to the next stage of human evolution when, hopefully, we can return to the more peaceful male-female partnership model but as evolved humans.

In Egypt a whole civilization built pyramids to overcome degeneration and death. They attempted to transform the pharaoh into a regenerating god, seeking eternal life.

In India the great yogis and teachers overcame the limitations of self-consciousness and achieved cosmic, universal consciousness through yoga, or union with the All. They revealed that God (Brahman) is the Supreme Spirit, the one infinite, eternal Presence — and that the manifestation of this Presence is the human Spirit or Self.

In Greece the human mind penetrated the veil of matter and intuited the structure of the atom. The rudiments of science were born, the science now leading our generation to the discovery of our own birth narrative and of nature's invisible creative technologies — the atom, the gene, the brain — bringing us to the threshold of cocreation or codestruction.

In Israel the great evolutionary idea was grounded in Abraham's covenant with God for the promised land, a new heaven and Earth, a new Jerusalem. Humans were in partnership with God for the transformation of the person and the world, through obedience to the Law. Life seemed to have a direction. Among the Jewish people a new expectation of the transformation of the material world arose, setting in motion the drive toward the next turn on the spiral.

Lao-tzu founded the Taoist religion in China, which is based on living in harmony with the great impersonal power (what we are calling the creative process of universal evolution). The sacred book of Taoism, *The Tao Te Ching*, teaches that heaven, Earth, and humans were created to be in harmony with one another, but that humans lost the way and created a world of disharmony.

Zoroaster, a Persian prophet, based his teaching on the one and only God, a supreme being of beauty, righteousness, and immortality.

Confucius believed in a supreme being, but placed the emphasis on our ethical relationships to one another to help us realize and understand the preordained harmony and justice of the universe.

Buddha achieved enlightenment and taught the Four Noble Truths: that reality is permeated with suffering; that attachment, or "thirst for permanence," is the cause of suffering; that the cessation of suffering is a possibility; and that there is a path that leads to the cessation of suffering.

Then, Jesus, born out of the vision and expectation of Israel, embodied the future human — beyond current *Homo sapiens* — with qualities now being awakened in us as we mature as imaginal cells. Jesus was an original cocreator. He demonstrated the power of being one with Source, incorruptible, with an unbroken connection to the process of creation, which he called Father, Abba, or intimate parent. His statement "I and my Father are one (John 10:30)," translated into evolutionary language, means "If you have seen me, you have seen the divine intelligence of the universe."

Jesus demonstrated the next stage of life with powers over the material world. He healed as easily as he breathed — effortlessly. He produced the loaves and the fishes in abundance. He calmed the weather. He revealed that through love of God and the other as oneself, he, and eventually we, could be radically transformed. We do not know what actually happened after the crucifixion, but the story tells us that he reappeared in a new body, resurrected, with continuity of consciousness — a body sensitive to thought. He promised that we would do the work he did and even greater work in the fullness of time. In the story he transcended the human condition, representing a quantum jump in one lifetime.

Paul told us that the sufferings of the present cannot be compared with the glory that shall be revealed in us. "Behold, I show you a mystery, but we shall not all sleep, we shall all be changed" (1 Cor. 15:51). John wrote in the Revelation of the new Jerusalem, "and death shall be no more, neither shall there be mourning, nor crying, nor pain anymore, for the former things have passed away . . . Behold I make all things new" (Rev. 21:4,5).

These incredible messages of the next stage of human evolution spread like wildfire throughout the dying pagan world. Those who resonated with this possibility formed small groups and set in motion the expectation of a new life, in some future time, which I believe to be our current time. Expectation creates reality. As we believe, so it is done unto us.

Later Mohammed began teaching the belief in one God and the attainment of peace through submission to the will of God. The spiritual template for the next stage of our evolution was established. As Michael Grosso wrote in *Frontiers of the Soul,*

> The perspective I adopt features an evolutionary view of religion. Looking back in time, people may learn to see the earliest spiritual visions of the human race in a new light. They may come to see that the first products of the spiritual imagination were projected images of their own evolutionary future. From this perspective all the gods and goddesses, indeed, the whole pantheon of spiritual powers, become images of super-evolved humanity.[7]

From the perspective of the new story of creation, the great mystics who founded the world's religions are embodiments of different aspects of the future human. At least one visionary mystic or leader patterned each culture and cultivated specific qualities we now need to realize the next stage of our evolution: the mindfulness of Buddha, the Tao or Way of Lao-tzu, the yoga of the Hindus, the love of God and the Law of the Jewish people, the faith and obedience to Allah of the Muslim people, the understanding of community and Earth of native peoples and the Goddess tradition of prehistoric times, and Jesus' promise of radical personal transformation through love of God and of the other as oneself. All these qualities, and many others, may be seen as evolutionary potentials in us, which are further activated as we approach the next turn on the spiral.

More recently, two new tools of our transformation appeared: the scientific method and democratic institutions. Science is the mind's understanding of the processes of creation, such as the atom, the gene, and the brain. We penetrated the veil of nature, as the early Greeks did, but with a scientific method of investigation that began to reveal how nature actually works so that we could enter the process of creation ourselves. Out of science came technology, beginning the shift, as Eric Chaisson put it, from "matter-dominance to life-dominance" as we learned the laws of nature. We can release the power at the heart of the atom and build in miniature atom by atom as nature does through nanotechnology. We can alter our genetic code and create new life forms in laboratories. We seek to understand and reprogram the clock of death that was set with multicellular life hundreds of millions of years ago. We are extending our life spans, building new body parts, and even attempting to transfer our consciousnesses into computers to recreate ourselves in an advanced silicon-based life, which some believe will carry the human species in a new form into the galaxies.

The second great tool of our transformation is democracy. In the same time that the scientific method arose the ideas of freedom were set forth, especially in the United States in the Declaration of Independence, the Constitution, and the Bill of Rights. The New World called to pioneering souls throughout the globe to experience their freedom to worship, to build, to earn their living, to become fully themselves. The next phase of human potential was activated: the individual was set free from the categories of class and religion. Democracy provided the social architecture for the awakening of individual creativity en masse, which is necessary for the next stage of our emergence. Democracy set the stage for the awakening of the imaginal cells and the beginning of the social potential movement.

Through science and democracy we gained the power to affect nature and transform the world. But through our successes we began to overpopulate Earth and to pollute our environment. We had no idea that there was a limit to growth. We were merely trying to preserve our lives and fulfill our dreams, following the two great human drives of self-preservation and reproduction. Few realized that we were heading for a global crisis of limits, that we would have to change our behavior or we would self-destruct.

We can have compassion for ourselves, for we did not know what the effect of our actions would be. Like those single cells in the seas of early Earth, we are running out of energy, resources, and space. We know that out of that crisis billions of years ago came multicellular life, the biosphere, the origin of the species, and us.

If we had been a rock on Earth before life began and someone had said, "You, rock, are going to get up and walk and talk and fly to the moon!" could we have believed it? Yet here we are with new capacities bursting the very bonds of Earth. Can we imagine what may be emerging from our struggle? The answer is yes, for we can learn from the lessons of the past and apply them to our evolution now. One of the great values of knowing our story is to remember the amazing capacity of evolution to create new forms out of old.

We can see our spiral as one continuous process of transformation. Each turning point on the spiral represents a breakthrough in consciousness and freedom. We can see the appearance of the great religions when sensitive humans were touched by the fire of Spirit at the core of the spiral, coming in contact directly with the designing intelligence running through the whole process. We see the core of the spiral as Spirit in action, the unmanifest manifesting in form, pressing each being to fulfill its potential and now breaking through in the minds of millions of humans, ready to more fully express Spirit in action in our own lives.

The Next Stage

The combination of science and democracy has led us toward the next stage of our evolution. The thinking layer of Earth, the

noosphere, has matured. Let's visualize it now: Gregory Stock wrote
in *Metaman,*

> The major evolutionary significance of humanity lies in the vast
> integrated entity it is creating rather than in the power of human
> beings as separated individuals.... Imagine looking down from
> the moon at the night side of an Earth pitch dark and invisible
> except for a brightly lit network of human constructions — lumi-
> nous cities, highways, canals, telephone and power lines. A faint,
> speckled web of light would seem to float in space. Some regions
> of this lacework would form intricate geometric patterns, others
> would seem random and disconnected. Far from inert, this dis-
> tant pattern of light would change and grow over decades, its
> shimmering fibers forming, extending, and joining in an almost
> vegetative fashion. This resemblance to life is not mere coinci-
> dence; the thin patina of humanity and its creation is truly a living
> entity. It is a "superorganism" — a community of organisms so
> fully tied together that it is a single living being...although
> human centered, it is more than just humanity. [It] is also the
> crops, livestock, machines, buildings, communications, transmis-
> sions, and other non-human elements and structures that are part
> of the human enterprise.[8]

We are the humans who happened to be born as the noosphere
connected and is on the verge of a collective awakening through us.
We are like cells in the body of an infant who is being born. We are
the ones who must consciously handle the fateful transition from
one phase of our evolution to the next.

Let's sense ourselves now in this moment, feeling around us the
crises of limits, the threat to our life-support systems, the pain of
hunger, fear, and injustice, the expansion of capacities, the desire for
self-expression, the search for a sense of direction and meaning —
all the confusion of this modern time. The process is speeding up

within us. Duane Elgin wrote in *Awakening Earth*,

> Because the pace of change is accelerating enormously, we should not assume that thousands or even millions of years will be required for us to achieve our initial maturity as a species. We have entered a time of explosive development...with each successive dimensional epoch there has been a dramatic collapse in the span of time required to move through a given stage.... Evolution is quickening at a truly remarkable pace.... In my judgment humanity has the potential to reach its initial maturity within another dozen generations, or roughly 500 years.[9]

Let's ask ourselves this key question: What is the significance of the next turn on the spiral? What is happening to us now?

CHAPTER FOUR

Our Crisis Is a Birth

et's rise up through the blue cocoon of Earth's atmosphere into the blackness of outer space and witness ourselves as one living system. Let's expand our sense of reality and see ourselves as members of one planetary body, struggling to coordinate ourselves as a whole. We see that we are gasping for breath as pollution chokes our lungs. We must handle our own wastes as toxins poison our air, our soil, our water, our bodies. We must shift to renewable, nonpolluting sources of energy. We feel the pangs of hunger increasing as population escalates and more and more of us are hungry. All around us our old life-support systems are breaking down. What worked before has become destructive. We do not have much time to change. We know that if we continue the behavior that worked so well in the past, we will destroy our chances for life.

This extraordinarily complex task has been thrust upon us for the first time in history, with "no operating manual for Space Ship Earth," as Buckminster Fuller put it.[1] Yet, despite our fear and ignorance, we are learning to manage a planetary system.

Our crisis is a birth. We are one living system and we have come to the limit of one phase of natural growth on a finite planet. In *The Life Era,* Eric Chaisson suggested that perhaps the reason we have not yet met other high-technology species is because there are none.[2] These decades we are now undergoing — when a species hits its growth limits and gains the technological powers to destroy itself — are so dangerous that, he surmised, perhaps no other species has survived the transition. This idea is called the principle of cosmic selection and is why we must learn ethical evolution quickly.

We are in the midst of a massive up-welling of human potential, creativity, anger, and frustration. We are confused and reactionary, yet bursting with new capacities... just like a newborn child. Or, we may see ourselves as planetary midwives helping to deliver ourselves as a planetary system toward our next stage of life. As we seek to facilitate a gentle birth, a graceful and nonviolent transition to the next stage of our evolution, we will discover a natural pattern, a design of our birth transition, and develop a plan to cooperate with this design.

The Period of Our Birth

Let's examine the period of our birth and a few of its salient events. As we noted, our labor pains began in 1945 with the explosion of the atomic bombs over Japan. This was a sign that the shift to the next stage of our evolution had begun: We would either evolve in consciousness or self-destruct our system.

Three key events stand out in the 1960s as critical to our birth transition. The first is the Apollo space program. Our species left the womb of Earth and set foot on the moon. We became physically universal in that we stepped beyond our biosphere and found on the moon and the asteroids the materials of a thousand Earths. Thus, solar energy and nonterrestrial materials could eventually provide resources for the physical growth of a universal species.

But the most immediate importance of the space program is not our potential for developing new resources and energy from space. It was seeing the great picture of ourselves taken from the moon. Our first baby picture! Seeing ourselves as one magnificent globe of life floating in the blackness of space triggered the second great event during the period of our birth: the awakening of the environmental movement. In 1970, only one year after the lunar landing, the first Earth Day occurred. Suddenly, millions of us fell in love with our Earth as a whole. We saw that the environment is not something separate from ourselves. It is our extended body. We are all connected. What the mystics had told us from time immemorial became a pragmatic fact. We are all members of this planetary body. We fell in love with ourselves as a whole. It was impossible to love our North and not our South, our East and not our West. A spontaneous joy coursed through the planet. People became passionately concerned about the trees, the air, the animals, the water, the ozone layer, and more. A growing number began to take responsibility for nature as a whole and for other species because they were part of ourselves. Our birth process matured as we struggled to preserve and evolve our life-support systems as well as coexist consciously and compassionately with other species.

The third crucial event of the 1960s is the awakening of women en masse to a new identity, a new function, a new role in evolution. Suddenly, in one generation we saw that our age-old function of massive reproduction had to stop. We began shifting from the all-consuming and heroic effort of birthing and nurturing five or ten children to the newer effort of finding self-expression and meaningful work — moving from the first two basic human drives for self-preservation and reproduction toward self-evolution and co-creation.

We seek now to fulfill our vast and yet untapped potential as individuals and as a species capable of conscious evolution. We are shifting from procreation to cocreation, from the effort of giving birth to our children to the equally demanding work of giving birth to our full potential selves. Feminine energy is being liberated by the population crisis to express itself for the sake of the larger human family and all life on Earth — and just in time. For in feminine creativity lie innovations, gifts, and vital contributions to our social potential movement and to the evolution of humanity.

In one extraordinary decade we learned that we are physically universal, and we recognized that we are all members of one planetary body and must care for ourselves as a whole. In addition, one-half the human race began to change its function from maximum procreation to something new! These events, along with many other significant breakthroughs, marked the period of our birth, comparable perhaps to the first few days after a biological organism is born.

Meanwhile, our planetary nervous system, our media, have begun to link us up as one interfeeling, interacting body. Although we may not always be aware of it, during this extended period there has been a continuous and massive effort to connect through our hearts. In 1985 "Live Aid," the television broadcast on the theme of hunger, connected us for 18 hours and was viewed by nearly 2 billion people. Compassion for the suffering of others awoke in our hearts as popular musicians sang Michael Jackson's "We are the world, we are the children."

John Randolph Price, in his book *The Planetary Commission*, asked for a "healing of this planet and to the reign of spiritual love and light in this world — with no less than 50 million (one percent of the human race) — meditating at the same time on December 31, 1986."[3] And the first World Healing Meditation occurred at noon Greenwich mean time.

If the universe is really more like a thought than a thing, as physicist John Wheeler has said, and if we are indeed the "universe in person," then we may say that the universe itself began to think the thought of peace and harmony on Earth. In 1987 the Harmonic Convergence sent millions to resonate with sacred places on Earth. At dawn people went to mountains, to groves, to parks, to pyramids, and to temples to empathize with the living Earth. Empathy for one another and for nature charged the global mind with love. During the event I was in Boulder, Colorado, with Jose Arguelles, the originator of the Harmonic Convergence. He said to me, "Barbara, the world will never be the same again."

In 1988 Gorbachev went to the United Nations and called for cooperation and even cocreation. No one can claim a direct cause and effect between mass events of love and peace and global change, but nonetheless it is true that the world was never the same again.

In the 1990s the Communist empire crumbled, falling of its own weight as people struggled to find their own way in freedom. The Berlin Wall came down. Television communicated the joy, the liberty, the hope to billions of us simultaneously. Celebration spread throughout the social body. Not predicted by leaders and experts, a nonviolent, people-motivated revolution had occurred. (Those who had been citizen diplomats in the Soviet Union meeting with its brilliant, creative people seeking freedom were not so surprised.)

Millions were liberated from the largest totalitarian dictatorship the world had seen. Communism was defunct, overcome, yet liberal democracy and capitalism were foreign systems, especially in Russia, and were also showing their limitations in the West. New social forms that might actually lead toward a more holistic, cooperative, freer world had not yet emerged. There was as yet no well-established third way between communism and capitalism. The social potential movement was still too young. Yet, movements for peace in Ireland and the Mideast grew. Apartheid fell in South Africa. New groups became empowered. The idea of equality of races and sexes, of ignored or suppressed minority groups gained respect. The very idea of war was seen as immoral, even though we still armed ourselves and fought.

But as the world became more integrated and dictators lost their grip, previously suppressed groups sought greater individualization. Each group, nation, culture, sexual preference, race, creed, and color wanted to assert its identity. The rise of nationalism, ethnicism, and political correctness surprised a world that many felt was ready to become a global village. We sought identity in our ethnic or racial roots and overlooked our common roots in the cosmos and our common destiny as a universal humanity. We did not see that we were on the threshold of a planetary birth, a next stage of human evolution. Instead, we became regressive and turned against ourselves, rather than looking forward together. Something vital was missing. There was — and still is — no common story or vision of the future to attract us.

Meanwhile, the United States has lost its enemy. The vast military-industrial-technological complex no longer has a common threat. It sits poised, with no mission equal to its immense evolutionary capacities. Global corporations of inordinate power span the Earth and mine its resources while the environment degrades and millions starve. The electronic media connect us, and the Internet allows us to communicate individually. It is a moment of transformation toward devolution or evolution.

The Collective Rise of Consciousness

Let's imagine that we are planetary diagnosticians, called in to assist in this period of our birth. What do we see? We find ourselves to be a brilliant species with artistic, spiritual, scientific, and technological genius. We are the jewel of our solar system, budding with genius and creativity, ready to grow. The vast majority of our members are good; we care for our young and strive to follow an ethic of consideration for others. Yet the history of our species is brutal, tragic in the cruelty we have afflicted upon one another, upon other species, and upon Earth herself. This flaw, this sense of separation from one another, from nature, and from Spirit, is the essence of evil.

Our situation has come to a critical stage. Are there some heretofore hidden processes in us that we could activate, some homeopathic remedies for our violence, that could stimulate more empathy, connectedness, and love?

Peter Russell estimated in *The Global Brain Awakens* that "10 billion seems to be the approximate number of units required in a system before a new level of evolution can emerge."[4] Coincidentally, it takes approximately 10 billion atoms to make a cell and 10 billion cells to make a brain. One more doubling of the human population will make 10 billion people, and this is expected in the lifetime of the present generations. Is 10 billion people what it takes for us to feel that we are all connected? But this is already a fact. We *are all* connected. Does it actually take a certain density of neurons on the planet for us to *feel* it and to overcome the illusion that we are separate from one another, from nature, and from the great creating process that is now flowing through us?

Here is a fascinating comparison with what happens to a newborn baby just after birth and what may happen to a planetary organism just after its birth period. At first the baby does not know that it has been born. Then, at some unexpected moment, after it has struggled to coordinate itself and nurse, stimulated by this effort its little nervous system links up and, suddenly, it opens its eyes and smiles at its mother. In that radiant smile it signals that it knows, at some deep level, that all is well, that it can survive and grow.

Here we are, from the perspective of the new creation story, a planetary species just after birth, struggling to coordinate ourselves as a whole, fearing the destruction of our life-support systems, confused, and afraid. Nonetheless, our planetary nervous system is linking us up through phones, faxes, global satellites, and the Internet. Are we being prepared for a time in the not too distant future when we will have an actual, empathic experience of our oneness? Are we possibly at the threshold, as a newly emerging planetary organism, of our first *planetary smile*, a mass linkup of consciousness now emerging in so many: an awareness that we are whole, we are one, we are good, we are universal? Is this sense of connectedness and wholeness a vital part of the design we can facilitate? I believe the answer is yes and that it can become the catalyst and be fostered by us, as shown later in this book.

Rupert Sheldrake, the British plant biologist, proposed in *A New Science of Life* that systems are regulated not only by the laws known to physical sciences, but also by invisible morphogenetic fields.[5] His theory suggests that if one member of a species performs a certain behavior, it affects all others ever so slightly. In a famous experiment rats trained to run a maze in one laboratory seemed to affect the learning rate of rats in a completely separate laboratory who learned to go through the maze more quickly after the first group did so. If a behavior is repeated long enough, its morphic resonance builds up and begins to affect the entire species. What began with the great mystics may be accelerating in us because of the crises and opportunities of our birth, thereby awakening the imaginal cells to their new potentials. We may have entered what Peter Russell called a phase of "superexponential growth, leading to a chain reaction, in which everyone suddenly starts making the transition to a higher level of consciousness." He wrote in *The White Hole in Time,*

> Could it be that in much the same way as the destiny of matter in a sufficiently massive star is to become a black hole in space, the destiny of a self-conscious species — should it be sufficiently full of love — is a "spiritual supernova?" Is this what we are accelerating toward? A moment when the light of inner awakening radiates throughout the whole? A white hole in time?[6]

Five Lessons of Evolution

To help answer Russell's questions and to discover the greater design of evolution, let's look backward to see if we can learn from the patterns of past quantum jumps to help us through the traumatic period of our birth and the next turn on the evolutionary spiral. By reviewing our new story, we gain five major lessons that will encourage us to move forward now. The historical perspective of a few thousand or even million years is not enough time to see the recurring patterns in cosmic evolution. When we stand back and witness the unfolding story — the big bang, Earth, life, animal life, early human life, and now another transformation — the logic of our hope is revealed, guidelines are given, and patterns of our transformation become visible.

1. Quantum transformations are nature's tradition. "Quantum" in this context means a jump from one state to the next that cannot be achieved through incremental change alone. The jump from nonlife to life or from the most intelligent animal to early human is

an example of quantum transformation. Infinitesimally small differences eventually lead to radical discontinuity and newness. The capacity of evolution to produce radical newness is truly astonishing. One hundred thousand years ago there were no *Homo sapiens*; a few millions ago there were no early humans. Before that there was no biosphere and no Earth, and 15 billion years ago there was no material universe. Nature works through radical change.

2. Crises precede transformation. When nature reaches a limitation, it does not necessarily adapt and stabilize; it innovates and transforms, as we saw with the single-cell crisis. Problems are often evolutionary drivers vital to our transformation. We learn to look for innovations that the problems are stimulating. We view our problems positively and notice the transformations occurring around us. For example, the threat of nuclear weapons is forcing the human race to go beyond war. The environmental crisis is awakening us to the fact that we are all connected and must learn how to manage a planetary ecology. We learn to expect the unexpected and to anticipate the new.

3. Holism is inherent in reality. Nature forms whole systems from separate parts. Subatomic particles form atoms, atoms form molecules, molecules form cells, cells form multicellular animals, on and on to humans — one of the most complex organisms on Earth, as Jan Smuts pointed out in his seminal work, *Holism and Evolution*.[7] We see that planet Earth is herself a whole system. We are being integrated into one interactive, interfeeling body by the same force of evolution that drew atom to atom and cell to cell. Every tendency in us toward greater wholeness, unity, and connectedness is reinforced by nature's tendency toward holism. Integration is inherent in the process of evolution. Unity does not mean homogeneity, however. Union differentiates. Unity increases diversity: We are

becoming ever more connected as a planet while we seek further individuality for our cultures, our ethnic groups, and our selves.

4. Evolution creates beauty, and only the beautiful endures. Every leaf, every animal, every body that endures is exquisite. Even creatures we may consider dangerous or disgusting are beautifully made. The process of natural selection favors elegant, aesthetic design. (This gives us courage as we recognize the crude forms of so many modern cities, houses, and machines.) If this tendency of nature continues through us, the creations of human nature will become ever more ephemeral, miniaturized, and beautiful.

5. Evolution raises consciousness and freedom. This lesson is the most important of all. Teilhard de Chardin called it "the law of complexity/consciousness."[8] As a system becomes more complex — from nonlife to life, from single cell to animal, from animal to human — it jumps in consciousness and freedom. Each is a jump through greater complexity. Our planetary system is becoming more complex. We are being connected by our media, our environment, our powers of destruction. If we drop a nuclear weapon on an "enemy," the fallout kills us. If a child starves in Africa or a youth is shot in Los Angeles, we feel it in our homes through television. This globalization is awakening in us a whole-system consciousness to complement the more mystical unitive or cosmic consciousness. This consciousness, a synthesis of both inner and outer connectedness, is still unstable in us, as perhaps self-consciousness and individual awareness was unstable in the animal world. Yet, the tendency toward expanded consciousness and freedom is the direction of evolution itself.

The five lessons of evolution provide a response to the crisis of meaning we face in this postmodern world. As business visionary Mark Donohue said to me,

Today we are beginning to discover a systems perspective to guide our new capacities, one that respects the 15 billion year history of successful transformation. Many of us realize that there is an implicate pattern of success, that we are not random events cast on the seas of time, that we are now cocreative with evolution itself. We no longer need to solely be reactive to our problems. We can be proactive and choose a future commensurate with our self-evident capacities.[9]

These lessons do not mean we will inevitably succeed. Evolution is a contingency, not an inevitability. We become potentialists, not optimists. We see the potential for evolution in the system, and in understanding our possibilities we take appropriate action. From this time forward, evolution proceeds more by choice than by chance.

The Next Turn on the Spiral

Currently, there is a wide range of opinion as to whether we are declining rapidly and perhaps irreversibly toward global environmental or economic catastrophe, or whether our crises are leading us toward a positive future. Both scenarios, as well as many variations, are possible. The purpose of this book is to discover a plausible positive scenario that attracts us to work toward it. For as we see reality, so we act, and as we act, so we tend to become.

The next turn on the evolutionary spiral is a quantum jump, yet there are signs that we are moving toward a positive future in the short range, which could make the transition from this stage of evolution to the next far less traumatic. For example, Peter Schwartz, a cofounder and chair of the Global Business Network and author of "The Art of the Long View," offered one possible scenario in the cover story in *Wired* magazine, July 1997,

We are watching the beginnings of a global economic boom on a scale never experienced before. We have entered a period of sustained growth that could eventually double the world's economy every dozen years and bring increasing prosperity for — quite literally — billions of people on the planet. We are riding the early waves of a 25-year run of a greatly expanding economy that will do much to solve seemingly intractable problems like poverty and to ease tensions throughout the world. And we'll do it without blowing the lid off the environment.... Historians will chronicle the 40-year period from 1980 to 2020 as the key years of a remarkable transformation. In the developed countries of the West, new technology will lead to big productivity increases that will cause high economic growth — actually, waves of technology will continue to roll out through the early part of the 21st century. And then, the relentless process of globalization, the opening up of national economies and the integration of markets, will drive the growth through much of the rest of the world.... These two metatrends — the fundamental technological change and a new ethos of openness — will transform our world into the beginnings of a global civilization, a new civilization of civilizations, that will blossom through the coming century.[10]

Universal Humanity

Universal Humanity

Let's imagine that such a positive trend is unfolding. The noosphere is maturing; we are appreciating our new story; cultural creatives are proliferating and connecting; new technologies show promise of providing nonpolluting, renewable energy; and new social systems are emerging that reinforce cooperation and creativity. Imagine that coming forth out of these advances is a quantum jump toward the next stage of our evolution. In

Creating Our Future, David Ellis recommended that we choose a long-range future, 500 to 1,000 years ahead, beyond even the lifetimes of our children's children.[11] In this exercise we free ourselves from self-imposed limits and allow our deeper evolutionary intuition and desire to rise to consciousness. This expression then forms a magnetic field to pull us forward toward what we choose. This future is ourselves revealed, our potential manifested. Our future pulses in us as the oak tree animates the acorn.

As we seek this vision, we have the lessons of evolution to guide us and show us that our evolution is the expression of a 15-billion-year trend toward higher consciousness, toward greater freedom through more complex order. We have the passionate desire within our hearts to be our full potential selves. If we can make it through this period of our birth, if enough of us can learn ethical evolution, the future for humanity would be unlimited. We can imagine that in the next 1,000 years humanity will be acting out the promise, first laid down in the early religions, for paradise, for a new heaven and a new Earth in our evolving world.

Here, we just catch glimpses of our potential to allure us, to charm us and beckon us forward to experience it. In the seeing comes the believing, comes the acting upon what we see. Our image of the future is instrumental in the evolution of the world. This is what *conscious* evolution means.

Join with me in choosing the best and most glorious future possible. Let's imagine the good we can do by working harmoniously. Each of us will see it differently, and each has a vital contribution to give. Later in the book we will flesh out these visions. Now, let's just catch a glimpse of ourselves as a universal humanity with our spiritual, social, and scientific capacities working toward higher consciousness and greater freedom through more complex order.

Coming Attractions

We can see that cosmic consciousness has been secured. Those peak moments of higher awareness we have felt in flashes throughout human history are now stabilized, as self-consciousness was stabilized in the animal world when humans first appeared. The new morphogenetic field eases our transition from self-centered to spirit-centered humanity. We are connected to Source, not as creatures but as cocreators. The universal intelligence that flows through every particle in the universe is now conscious in us.

Through a combination of medical advances and the healing arts we are fully in touch with our body-minds and are becoming self-healing and self-regenerating. The extraordinary powers of mystics and healers are a normal capacity in all of us.

Our extended electronic nervous system has linked us up as one inter-feeling, interacting body. The global brain has turned on, and each of us has access to the knowledge of the whole system. Our intelligence has taken a quantum turn.

Our infant space programs have matured. As once the process of photosynthesis created the biosphere, now humans are creating the "humansphere" in outer space. As we reach our growth limits on Earth, we preserve and conserve life here while learning to extend life beyond our home planet. NASA engineer Kenneth Cox suggested a Third Millennium intention,

> To create a permanent living presence throughout the solar system and seek value and meaning for humankind in Earth/Space. To establish human settlements in Earth orbit, on planetary surfaces, and in other appropriate orbital space. To live, work, and prosper in multiple space communities in the solar system, and develop a virtual presence beyond our "local Earth-Moon-Sun universe." [12]

The stabilization of unitive consciousness combined with the extension of human habitats in space, increased intelligence through our maturing global brain with enhanced health and life extension supported by new technologies for nonpolluting energy such as solar-, hydrogen-, and vacuum-based energy, synergistic, win-win social systems and other innovations will radically alter the human condition. These capacities will be the conditions in which the social potential movement comes to fruition. Each person born into this extended spiritual, social, and physical environment will be a member of universal humanity. Our vast, untapped human potential will be called forth in an enriched noosphere as we engage in utterly new vocations and functions in the evolving social body. All of us will be free to be and do our best.

What is in store for us, if we can make it through this crisis of our birth, will make our hearts leap with joy now. It is a vision of the birth of a universal species, a quantum jump from *Homo sapiens* to *Homo "universalis,"* from the self-conscious human to the cosmic conscious, cocreative human.

Is it possible? Yes.

Can we do it? It depends on what you and I do now, in the next few decades, in this most critical period following our birth. We are on the threshold of *conscious* evolution — the next vital element in the life design.

PART II

CONSCIOUS EVOLUTION:
A NEW WORLDVIEW

CHAPTER FIVE

Conscious Evolution

Deep in the hidden process of our metamorphosis we can see a natural design — an evolutionary pattern to guide us toward the next stage of transformation. We intuit the presence of the still-invisible societal butterfly, yet how do we become it? What we are seeking is a worldview that will call forth our creative action and direct our immense powers toward life-oriented and evolutionary purposes. That guiding worldview is, I believe, conscious evolution. It holds that through our unprecedented scientific, social, and spiritual capacities we can evolve consciously and cocreatively with nature and the deeper patterns of creation (traditionally called God), thus enabling us to manifest a future commensurate with our unlimited species and planetary potential.

Conscious evolution as a worldview began to emerge in the latter half of the 20th century because of scientific, social, and technological abilities that have given us the power to affect the evolution of life on Earth. Conscious evolution is a metadiscipline; the purpose of this metadiscipline is to learn how to be responsible for the ethical guidance of our evolution. It is a quest to understand the processes of developmental change, to identify inherent values for the purpose of learning how to cooperate with these processes toward chosen and positive futures, both near term and long range.

This worldview is the fruit of all human history and the opening of the next stage of human development. It has come into focus midway in the life cycle of our planet with the maturation of the noosphere. Conscious evolution is awakening in imaginal cells as a vision of a new life to come and a desire to fulfill unique creativity in the cocreation of that new life.

The Second Great Event

As mentioned earlier, conscious evolution heralds the second great event in the history of the universe. We are not speaking of some minor new idea but of an advance in the evolution of evolution itself. Eric Chaisson wrote in *ZYGON,*

> Technologically competent life differs fundamentally from lower forms of life. We are different because we have learned to tinker not only with matter but also with evolution. Whereas previously the gene and the environment (be it stellar, planetary, geological, or cultural) governed evolution, we humans on planet Earth are rather suddenly gaining control of both these agents of change.... We now stand at the verge of manipulating life itself, potentially altering the genetic makeup of human beings [and even cloning ourselves]. We are, in fact, forcing a change in the way things change.... The emergence of technologically intelligent life on Earth, and perhaps elsewhere, heralds a whole new era, a Life Era. Why? Because technology, for all its pitfalls, enables life to begin to control matter, much as matter evolved to control radiative energy more than 10 billion years ago.

Though a mature Life Era may never come to pass, one thing seems certain: Our generation on planet Earth, as well as any other neophyte technological life forms populating the universe, is now participating in an astronomically significant transformation. We perceive the dawn of a whole new reign of cosmic development, an era of opportunity for life forms to begin truly to fathom their role in the cosmos, to unlock the secrets of the Universe, indeed to decipher who we really are and whence we came.... The implications of our newly gained power over matter are nothing short of cosmic.... As sentient beings we are currently beginning to exert a weighty influence in the establishment of a "universal life" with all its attendant features, not least of which potentially include species immortality and cosmic consciousness.[1]

The capacity for conscious evolution means that our species has become capable of understanding and resonating with the processes of creation itself. Already we can fathom the miracle of cosmogenesis — the story of the evolution of the cosmos. We can reach into the heart of nature and see the invisible workings of creation — the atom, gene, brain, ecological systems, stars, and galaxies. Spiritually we are attuning to the patterns of evolution within us as we begin to transcend the illusion of separation born out of the phase of *self-conscious* humanity.

Whether or not there is other life in the universe, our role, if we learn conscious evolution, is to become partners in the process of creation, enhancing life on Earth and bringing Earth's life into the universe. We rightly stand in awe of the magnificence of cosmogenesis as well as in reverence for ourselves as creatures of this monumental process.

As Catholic scholar Beatrice Bruteau wrote in "Symbiotic Cosmos," in a chapter entitled "Holy Technology,"

From having felt completely at the mercy of the natural world, we begin gradually to feel in a position of power over the natural world. There is a third stage of this development, and that is the sense of the natural world itself producing beings that can so intelligently and freely and creatively manipulate the natural world. We ourselves are products of the self-making world, and what we do by our technologies is continue the self-making of this world. When the technologically changed environment has in turn changed us, then we must see that this also is part of the self-making of the world.

Human extensions by means of technology are not to be opposed to "Nature." They are themselves part of what Nature is doing. It is the Cosmos itself, as the human being, that is doing these things as its own autopoietic (self-creating) development... and there is nothing riskier than creating a world so that it can grow up to be free and creative itself — I think that we must see our technology as something holy, as part of — at the moment, the vital advancing edge of the autopoetic, symbiotic cosmos.[2]

There is no hubris in the concept of conscious evolution — no pride that humans alone, by willful decision for selfish ends, with no regard for the laws of nature or the relationship with other species, can guide the process of change. We can clearly see that such self-centered behavior will destroy us. Conscious evolution inspires in us a mysterious and humble awareness that we have been created by this awesome process of evolution and are now being transformed by it to take a more mature role as cocreators. In this view we do not stand apart from nature, but, rather, we are nature evolving.

Nor is the concept anthropocentric. From the perspective of conscious evolution, *Homo sapiens*, in our current phase, is a transitional species. We are not viable in this state of separated consciousness with so much power. We will either evolve or become extinct.

Yet, we are advancing toward conscious evolution with every new discovery made by the collective efforts of hundreds of thousands of individuals. In the biological revolution, the healing arts, in humanistic, transpersonal, and spiritual psychologies of growth, in social innovations in the fields of health, education, and the media, in business, science, and the arts we are learning new abilities to cocreate with nature. And we are doing so based on human nature's intentional motivation, not as the passive experiencer but as the conscious codesigner of evolution.

The History of Quantum Change

How do we know that conscious evolution is the next quantum jump? We don't. Yet we do know, from the history of quantum transformations, that such radical change will eventually occur. Our evolutionary history has a long heritage of astonishing innovations. Let us remember, it is the nature of nature to transform, especially when life hits a growth limit.

I believe that the capacity for conscious evolution is a design innovation comparable in importance to other major evolutionary innovations. Let's briefly review the extraordinary history of quantum changes through design innovations, to gain a deeper insight into the potential of our capacity.

The design innovation that formed matter and Earth was the synthesis of the elements — from hydrogen and helium to iron and gold. It took billions years for nature to create a way to synthesize radiative energy to form the metals and minerals that make up our bodies today. Out of formless, shimmering gasses and explosions of supernovas the elements were formed, condensing light and motion into matter and providing the substance of all subsequent evolution.

For the origin of human life, the design innovation was the

genetic code — DNA intelligence — the exquisitely complex information at the heart of every cell coded with instructions that build our bodies. This nearly invisible information system coiled in the strands of our DNA holds the memory of the entire evolution of life and, some believe, the coding for further life to come. Timothy Leary stated the controversial hypothesis in *Info-Psychology: A Manual on the Use of the Human Nervous System According to the Instructions of the Manufacturers,*

> The DNA code contains the blueprint of the *past and the future.* The caterpillar DNA contains the design for construction and operation of the butterfly body. Geneticists are just now discovering "unused" sections of the DNA, masked by *histones* and activated by non-histone proteins, which are thought to contain the blueprint of the future. Evolution is not a blind, accidental, improvising process. The DNA code is a prospective blueprint which can be deciphered.[3]

Only since the 1950s, when the language of DNA was deciphered, have we known how the complex process of building our body-minds was accomplished. The awesome intelligence at the nucleus of every cell guides embryogenesis from a fertilized egg through birth, maturation, and death. (Rupert Sheldrake's new theory of morphic resonance, mentioned earlier, hypothesizes that there is more to it than instructions from DNA — suggesting there may be an invisible field that holds the experience of all members of a species.)

One of the critical design innovations for the biosphere and multicellular life was the process of photosynthesis, which occurred hundreds of millions of years ago, and transformed our barren planet into a living biosphere.

The design innovation that allowed the emergence of *Homo sapiens* from the animal world was language, culture, and the ability to communicate exo-genetically — outside the genetic code. In *Science and Sanity* Alfred Korzybski called this ability "time-binding" — the capacity to pass on information to one another through language, symbols, arts, and music.[4] Whereas biological evolution takes millions of years, cultural and social evolution takes place within hundreds of years and now at a faster pace — only decades. Through language, each generation learns from the one before, vastly accelerating the process of change. Language and culture built the noosphere, just as the process of photosynthesis and biological organisms — plants, animals, insects — built the biosphere.

Conscious evolution is the next design innovation. It is based on our ability to understand the innovations of the past, such that we can consciously codesign our future, drawing on the knowledge of how nature formed matter, how DNA intelligence works, how photosynthesis occurs, how ecological systems are maintained, and how language and culture affect us. Conscious evolution is a natural extension of the ongoing process of evolutionary innovations leading to greater awareness, freedom, and capacity.

The new worldview already exists in an early stage. There is a large and growing body of knowledge in almost every arena — science, psychology, cosmology, art, literature, philosophy, and business — but there is not a definable field called conscious evolution to coordinate all the separate insights. Our fledgling worldview is still almost invisible, yet it is drawing to it brilliant minds in every field and function who hold the mysterious sense of hope for the future.

CHAPTER SIX

Exploring the Meaning of Conscious Evolution

It is important to realize how radically new the concept of conscious evolution is. As an emerging worldview it is no more than 50 years old because the primary conditions that brought it into existence are themselves only that recent. This newness explains why it has not yet been incorporated into our academic, political, and religious worldviews.

There are three new elements vital to conscious evolution. I call them "the three Cs": new cosmology, new crises, and new capacities.

1. New Cosmology

Our understanding of cosmogenesis has brought forth a new vision of all creation. It was only in the mid-1960s that two scientists, Arno Penzius and Robert Wilson, identified background radiation from the original moment of creation — the big bang — and were able to extrapolate backward in time to those first instants of creation.

"What they were hearing was nothing less than the vibration of the birth of the universe," wrote Richard Elliott Friedman in *The Disappearance of God: A Divine Mystery.*[1]

Theodore B. Roszak wrote in *The Voice of the Earth,*

> The universe has altered radically over time. It has a history. These findings — background radiation, the quasar, the big bang, and later Stephen Hawking's research on black holes — rapidly coalesced with quantum mechanics and Einstein's relativity to produce a radically new world picture. We now know that history is the characteristic of everything, not only living things. We know that the heavier elements we are made of were forged during that history in the deep interior of stars. We know that whatever exists, no matter how intricate, has to be accounted for within the dynamics of cosmic expansion and the framework of cosmic time.[2]

Anyone born before the 1960s was not educated in the crucial new idea that the physical universe had a beginning in time, has been evolving for billions of years, and is still evolving now through us as well as throughout the entire cosmos. When I went to college in the early 1950s, I was told that the frontiers of knowledge had been mostly closed. Neither our new creation story nor the new worldview was even considered at that time.

The importance of the new cosmology is that we recognize the universe has a history and a direction and, therefore, so do we. It reinforces the new story. The metapattern that connects everything is involved not only in living systems but in the entire process of creation. The universe has been evolving in time toward ever more complex systems with ever greater freedom and consciousness. There has been a cosmological phase, from the big bang to the first cell; a biological phase, from the first cell to the first human; a noological phase, from the first human to us. And now, we are entering a cocreative phase, when human life becomes consciously coevolutionary with nature.

The idea that there is a history to everything is a fundamental component in conscious evolution. It reinforces our desire to evolve in history rather than purely metaphysically, or in another afterworld, yet helps us see the future not as more of the same, but as radically new and self-transcending, fulfilling our deepest aspirations for transformation. It gives us long-range visions not only of our past, some 15 to 20 billion years ago, but of our future, which is estimated to continue 100 billion years beyond our lifetimes.

This immense scope of time relieves us from any sense of limitation and gives us hope that in some form our species can have an ever-evolving future. We have a new sense of identity, not as isolated individuals in a meaningless universe, but rather as the universe in person, cocreators of the next stage of our evolution. We can see that past design innovations such as the synthesis of matter, the DNA code, photosynthesis, and language have led to the new design innovation, conscious evolution.

2. New Crises

Our new crises is another vital element to conscious evolution, especially the environmental crisis. From the perspective of the new story, this complex crisis can be understood as a natural but dangerous stage in the birth process of a universal humanity.

We are undergoing the shift in a planetary birth. As we have already seen, what worked before will now destroy us. We must rapidly stop doing what we have done so successfully — building, overpopulating, polluting, and using up nonrenewable resources to survive. We know that cataclysms have wiped out whole species: 98 percent of all species became extinct before humans appeared.

But never before did a species know ahead of time that it might self-destruct and that it had an option to do something about it. Now we are shifting from reactive response to proactive choice. Our crisis is an evolutionary driver awaking us to the necessity and opportunity to choose a future commensurate with our potential and to take responsibility for our actions.

I believe that collectively, we do know how to coordinate ourselves as a whole, how to handle our waste, shift to renewable resources, and awaken to our unique, new roles in the maturation of our species. If the crisis is natural, so is the response.

The newness of the crisis means, however, that no existing leader or institution can train us. No team is waiting at the end of the birth canal, as far as we know! The process of awakening comes from our deeper and more intuitive knowing combined with scientific understanding.

3. New Capacities

Our new capacities — powers now available to us, such as biotechnology, nuclear power, nanotechnology, cybernetics, artificial intelligence, and artificial life — are radical evolutionary capacities that are potentially dangerous in our current state of self-centered consciousness. From our current perspective they may seem unnatural, and indeed they are. Yet, if we consider our needs at the next stage of evolution — as a universal species — these may be precisely the abilities we require to survive and grow in the extended physical environment of outer space, and in the expanded consciousness environment of inner space.

In a biological organism, however, capacities that are lethal in the womb are vital in the world. So our extraordinary new powers, which can be deadly to us in our current stage of self-centeredness and planet-boundedness, may be natural for us at the next stage of cosmic consciousness and universal life.

Because we fear the danger of our new technologies in the present, we must not prematurely destroy them. Rather, we should see ahead to their possible use at the next stage of evolution and guide their application toward the emancipation of our evolutionary potential rather than attempting the impossible task of stopping knowledge and preserving the status quo. We must remember that the nature of nature is to transform — especially when nature hits a crisis of limits.

From the perspective of the three Cs, we can see that the new cosmology can be interpreted as the story of the birth of a universal humanity, that our new crises are the results of our natural birth process, and that our new capacities are the growing powers of a young, universal species — all barely one generation old.

Learning Conscious Evolution

How do we become conscious of conscious evolution? How does the new worldview penetrate the essence of our being and animate our actions? The key assumption here is that there is a natural pattern for the development of a planetary system, just as there is for a biological system. This pattern resides in the integration of the fields of knowing — spiritual, social, and scientific/technological.

1. Spiritual Conscious Evolution

The spiritual aspect of conscious evolution gives us access to that deeper pattern within us. We become conscious of the evolutionary impulse — the deeper pattern of creation — through inner guidance, motivation, intuition. It is the feeling within us urging us to be more, to know more, to reach out and touch, to activate our genius, to find our life purpose.

In conscious evolution, our spiritual experience expands to include resonance with the design of evolution. Our spiritual growth awakens our social potential, pressing us deeper inward to pick up that design and outward to express our creativity in the world through vocation. We work from within ourselves toward higher consciousness, greater freedom, and more complex order to effect a change in the world, first and foremost through our personal evolution.

With conscious evolution we are on the threshold of a cocreative spirituality as we learn to attune to the deeper patterns of creation. The lives of great avatars were transformed by resonance with deeper reality. Now, because of the rise of consciousness in ourselves, our lives can also be lifted up, not as saints or seers, but as humans at the next stage of our natural evolution — as imaginal cells, cocreative with the processes of evolution.

In *Design of Evolution*, Eric Jantsch coined a beautiful word to describe this expanding form of spiritual awareness: "syntony." He compared syntony to a way of knowing through resonance, or harmonizing with that which we seek to know. Perhaps as within our cells RNA (ribonucleic acid) is able to resonate with DNA, the genetic code, to pick up its pattern or frequency, then to go forth and assemble the proteins required to build the cell according to the DNA's design. Jantsch wrote,

> Syntony, which seems to be due to direct communication of individual human consciousness through some resonance process, seems to exhibit the same characteristics of holographic communication that seem to govern genetic information and brain functions.... As we have learned, though not too well, to design social

roles, we shall have to learn now to design systems of syntony, this implies a shift of focus from the rational level through the mythological to the evolutionary level of inquiry.[3]

In summary, the first way of accessing conscious evolution is to deliberately cultivate the capacity for inner knowing — syntony — spiritual resonance with the patterns of creation. We use our innate abilities to receive intuition, to act upon it, to accept feedback from the outside world, receiving further guidance, reaching out to test the guidance again and again until we learn to act spontaneously and directly from whole system intelligence.

2. Social Conscious Evolution

As we gain deeper alignment with the patterns of creation, we sadly see a world that is out of alignment. We see systems that are breaking down, causing misery, alienation, and violence almost everywhere. This breakdown is natural from the point of view that we are undergoing a birth process. Just as the systems of biological organisms break down and repattern themselves after birth, so our social systems, designed for the old phase of development, are now inadequate for the next phase and must repattern themselves.

Through conscious evolution we realize, for the first time as a species, that it is our responsibility to proactively design social systems that are in alignment with the tendency in nature toward higher consciousness, greater freedom, and more synergistic order. With our increase in freedom because of our new powers comes a commensurate increase in responsibility for the use of those powers. We no longer accept our society and its ills as a given; we become proactive, social cocreators and the social potential movement awakens. Not only a few outstanding social activists or leaders participate, but millions of so-called ordinary people in myriad organizations, projects, and initiatives undertake the work of healing and evolving our world.

For example, we need a sustainable, regenerative economy that takes into account that we are one planetary system in which we are all vital members, integrated in an environment that is part of our body, in a social system that frees us to express our life purpose in creative work. We need a new health care system that reinforces responsibility and self-healing. We need a mature media that communicates growth potential and the *new* news of our innovations and successes. We need a new form of self-governance that truly involves all of us in a deeper responsibility for ourselves and others, a genuine "higher self" governance. These are all parts of the enormous task of the social potential movement, yet we are blessed with the resources and intelligence to do it because so many of us have started to live our life purpose and desire to express our creativity in the world.

We can begin to build a new world by identifying and connecting the best innovations that embody the evolutionary perspective. Gary Zukav, one of the many pioneers, is exploring new social structures and systems in his forthcoming book *Universal Human.* Gary wrote in a personal letter that his new book is about,

> ...the interpersonal structures, such as marriage, and the social structures such as governance, education, health, science, and art that are emerging through multisensory humanity will replace those structures that are disintegrating.[4]

As the spiritual aspect of conscious evolution requires the deepening of our inner sensitivity to the patterns of creation, so the social aspect requires us to learn how to form social systems into which we can enter as individuals and sense that we are a vital and loving part of a whole. Rather than addressing this question from the outside — as changes that must be made in society "out there" — the social potential movement attempts to discover the synergistic, win-win social patterns from the inside. This discovery is made through integration of our body, mind, and spirit, through spiritual attunement with the patterns that connect, through our intimate relationships with one another, through learning how to relate as partners rather than as dominators, through understanding ecological and biological natural systems, and through our vocations. New social designs come forth from our deeper understanding of nature, human nature, and systems in resonance with the patterns in the process of creation, as described extensively in Hazel Henderson's book, *Building a Win-Win World*, and in the work of Elisabet Sahtouris, most recently in her article "The Biology of Globalization,"

> The globalization of humanity is a natural, biological, evolutionary process. Yet we face an enormous crisis, because the most central and important aspect of globalization, its economy, is currently being organized in a manner that so gravely violates the fundamental principles by which healthy living systems are organized that it threatens the demise of our whole civilization.[5]

Perhaps it is a matter of timing. It was not possible to create harmonious societies at any large scale, beyond the relatively peaceful tribal cultures, until the events of the last decades — the period of our birth — just as it is not possible for a fetus to get up and walk. Perhaps the great visions of new societies could not have been realized until we passed through the events we are still undergoing, which include:

- the maturation of the noosphere, which gives us the technical and social capacity to produce in abundance, to prolong our lives, to live in freedom, to be educated, to have mobility, and to have free choice of vocation

- the awakening of a critical mass of imaginal cells, or evolving humans, able to attune to the processes of evolution within themselves, moving from self-centered toward whole-centered consciousness and action

- reaching the limits to growth on a finite planet, learning how to shift to renewable and eventually fully abundant resources and energy, whether through fusion, solar energy, free energy from the vacuum field, or other possibilities

- the shift from procreation to cocreation, freeing the creativity of women from the enormous task of massive reproduction to give their loving energy to chosen children and to the larger human family while liberating men from the burden of feeding and protecting large families

Perhaps the utopian visions that have arisen for hundreds if not thousands of years are accurate precognitions of coming evolutionary possibilities. Perhaps these visions could not come true until we matured to the next stage of our evolution, the process we are undergoing now.

We have been young *Homo sapiens*, the big-brained creature that knows it knows, with an immortal spirit in a degenerating body, living in environments of scarcity, working ceaselessly to survive, and dying young. In the future, we can become universal humanity — cocreators, producing abundance for all in a universal environment with extended life spans and greater opportunity for individual expression. The actualization of these social visions has required the maturation of humanity to the stage of conscious evolution.

3. Scientific and Technological Conscious Evolution

Through molecular biology, nanotechnology, artificial intelligence, robotics, astronautics, and genetics, combined with the noetic science of consciousness, we are shifting from matter-dominance to life-dominance. The collective human intelligence has penetrated the invisible veil of nature to understand nature's processes and technologies of creation. As we understand the nature of matter as energy and information in motion, we become less dominated by it and more able to influence matter consciously.

Each scientist and technologist is part of a vast invisible web of hundreds of thousands of others, all drawing on the shared noosphere built by the genius of the past and by those in the present who are working in countless laboratories around the globe. Every advance made in the world is quickly communicated to other parts of the world. Through this collective capacity we are consciously entering the process of nature. We have taken a step toward Chaisson's "Life Era," in which technologically competent humans are gaining an understanding of matter, thereby changing the nature of evolution itself. Instead of seeing technology as merely useful or possibly destructive, we see it as the natural extension of nature's technologies, giving human nature the capacity to evolve evolution itself from unconscious to conscious.

Now that we are learning to evolve consciously, science and technology, along with all other disciplines, must learn to apply values to guide the use of these tremendous new capacities. If we accept an evolutionary agenda as the overarching goal in the Third

Millennium, then our scientific and technological brilliance will be naturally guided in that direction. We must learn to value scientific innovations crucial to nonlinear, quantum progress. For example, we know that solar energy will be a major energy resource within the next 100 years. Yet, society has not broadly supported this design innovation because of its short-term, consumption-based mentality. We must begin to see the depth and breath of our unborn history and let the self-evident lessons of evolution proactively guide our scientific and technological genius.

Science and technology cannot establish its goals alone, however, any more than the military or economic sectors can. It is only through the full-scale activation of a social potential movement that these systems will evolve.

If we can learn to combine our advanced technological capacities with an evolved spirituality and the ability to design synergistic social systems, we will be part of a quantum transformation, a jump as great as the jump from Neanderthal to *Homo sapiens.*

Conscious evolution is the design innovation that empowers us to become a universal humanity. We are crossing the evolutionary divide between creature and cocreator.

CHAPTER SEVEN

The Fabric of Civilization

onscious evolution is the new worldview vital to ethical evolution. It is a "meme" to guide us through this dangerous period toward an unlimited future. Memes are ideas woven into complex thought systems that organize human activities according to a specific pattern. The way genes build bodies, memes build cultures, societies, and the noosphere.

Howard Bloom beautifully described memes in his book, *The Lucifer Principle*:

> The meme is a self-replicating cluster of ideas. Thanks to a handful of biological tricks, these visions become the glue that holds together civilizations, giving each culture its distinctive shape. Genes sit at the center of each cellular blob, dictating the construction of a multi-billion-celled body like yours and mine. As genes are to the organism, so memes are to the super-organism — the noosphere — pulling together millions of individuals into a collective creature of awesome size. Memes stretch their tendrils through the fabric of each human brain, driving us to coagulate in the cooperative masses of family, tribe, and nation.[1]

Memes and Society

Memes are the most powerful force in human society. They guide our actions, build our societies, and organize our world. Just as genes are selected based on their ability to survive, so too, memes are selected for their viability.

In recent history we have seen certain memes gain enormous power, then disintegrate almost completely. For example, Nazism was a vicious meme that gripped the German people, stimulating them to commit acts that are unthinkable to virtually all Germans now. Daniel Jonah Goldhagen wrote in *Hitler's Willing Executioners: Ordinary Germans and the Holocaust,* "Germany during the Nazi period was inhabited by people animated by beliefs about Jews that made them willing to become consenting mass executioners...."[2] When the Nazis were defeated, that meme dissolved (or became recessive, since it still festers under the surface like a virus ready to infect the social memetic code). People changed their behavior, radically. Modern German society cannot conceive of burning, torturing, enslaving, starving, or exterminating millions of people.

The German people were not intrinsically bad — they were consumed by a diabolic meme. This reason does not excuse or justify, for ultimately, we are responsible for the memes we allow to guide us. The problem is, we usually don't know we have a meme, or rather, that a meme has us. Typically, we accept the consensual worldview without even noticing it. Conscious evolution teaches us to be meme conscious and create life-affirming memes that foster a positive future.

Communism was another recent worldview, or memetic code, that directed the energies and actions of millions for nearly a century. Karl Marx and Frederick Engel's economic philosophy was adapted by Lenin and the Bolsheviks, who eventually destroyed whole classes of people in the name of an ideal of a new society. Like Nazism, Communism, although born of an ideal, proved to be a lethal meme. It did not take into account human freedom and dignity, and it undermined the moral, spiritual, and productive capacities of a great people.

The meme of conscious evolution, given modern communications, could spread very quickly. Within a few decades it could become the guiding meme. Howard Bloom wrote in *The Lucifer Principle,*

> The meme of Christianity restructured the Roman Empire a mere 300 years after Jesus completed his Sermon on the Mount. Similarly, Marxism radically altered the shape of Russian society a startling 60 years after Karl [Marx] the cantankerous ambled out of the British Museum's library with the final manuscript of *Das Kapital* tucked tightly under his arm.[3]

When a meme no longer seems to explain the nature of reality or guides us toward goals that satisfy our deepest desire, it recedes or quickly becomes extinct. For example, prior to Gorbachev's glasnost and perestroika that started in the mid-1980s, Communists proclaimed that their ideology was the best in the world. By 1990 it was difficult to find anyone who believed in that authoritarian system. Former proponents denounced the dying meme, claiming they always knew it was wrong, just as Germans denounced Nazism.

Now that the meme of Communism has disintegrated, people who had been controlled by it are confused and disoriented. Western capitalism and liberal democracy are alien memes to them and tend to be rejected, much like a transplanted organ in the human body is often rejected. When healthy memes don't exist, however, recessive memes can resurface and take over, such as extreme nationalism or racial and ethnic hatred. It is very dangerous for a culture to be without a healthy meme.

The demise of Nazism and Communism has forced us to look at our own situation. Some of the most precious memes in the Western world are fading rapidly. Their passing has left us seemingly without shared values and a common awareness of life purpose. For example, the story told in the Gospels is no longer *literally* believable for millions. The worldview, or meme, of biblical literalism is dissolving in light of both scientific and historical research. Cosmologists know the world was not built in seven days. Historical scholars assert that Jesus said only a fraction of the adages in the Gospels. Scriptural narratives contradict one another and may not be based on historical fact but on faith, myth, and mystery. According to some scholars, the Gospels are a collection of great stories, insights, and spiritual truths compiled by a community of Jewish people inspired by one man of extraordinary, godlike qualities. Bishop John Shelby Spong suggested in *Liberating the Gospels*[4] that these people attempted to tell the story of his life in such a way as to conform to Jewish scripture and prophesy. Whatever the historical facts may be, it is increasingly difficult for many people to believe the stories exactly as they were written. Although a spiritual understanding of scripture is deepening in many, the undermining of the Gospels' literal interpretation is subtly shaking the foundation of the Western world. Values, morals, faith, hope, and charity have always been guided by this meme.

As the foundations of western Christendom are challenged by the new revelations of history and cosmology, so science itself is required to mature under the impetus of its own magnificent intelligence. The meme that rose to displace biblical literalism was scientific materialism. But this meme is also declining and along with it the story of inevitable progress through scientific and technological knowledge that has prevailed for the last 300 years. This powerful story and the memes that support it no longer stand unchallenged. The memes that describe matter, eternal time, and random chance, the basis of the scientific worldview, no longer fit the facts as revealed by scientific investigation. Matter has been dematerialized to the point of taking on certain attributes of mind. Eternal time has given way to duration and the directional unfolding of evolution in specific time frames, and chance could not be responsible for the complex order in the universe given the fact that there is no eternal time. For example, it seems incredible, statistically, that the universe could have been organized to its current degree of complexity in only 15 billion years. Theodore Roszak wrote in *The Voice of the Earth,*

> In the late 1970s Fred Hoyle and Chandra Wickramasinghe calculated the odds that life could have originated from just such an undirected sloshing about. Rather than trying to compute the probability for an entire organism springing into existence, they limited the problem to a sequence of twenty or thirty key amino acids in the enzymes of some hypothetical cell. The number they came up with was one chance in $10^{40,000}$. [5]

Ken Wilber wrote in *A Brief History of Everything,*

> Something more than chance is pushing the universe. For traditional scientists, chance was their salvation. Chance would explain all. Chance, plus unending time would produce the universe. But they don't have unending time, and so their god fails them miserably. That god is dead. Chance is not what explains the universe; in fact, chance is exactly what the self-transcending drive of the Kosmos overcomes. [6]

The meme of individualistic democracy, although still the best of all existing systems of governance, is incomplete as a guiding idea. We, in the United States, need only to look in our streets, jails, and homeless shelters to see the results of excessive individualism in a commercialized world. Arthur Schlesinger described it as the "dis-uniting of America," as ethnic, religious, sexual, racial, and other special interest groups fortify themselves by putting others down.[7] Most especially, we see the loss of community, the breakup of the family, and the alienation and self-destructive violence among the young. The meme of secular, liberal democracy is good, but not sufficient. Reactionary or conservative response, however, is not the answer. Although conservatism is an effort to reaffirm personal responsibility and creativity, it lacks a new vision and a new social architecture to foster both cooperation and responsibility.

Our goal cannot be to return to the past, nor can it be to move forward to a future that is more of the same. A vast array of positive social innovations leading to reintegration of community, participatory management, and economic reforms is now helping us work toward a new level of cooperation and community. The full expression of this emerging leadership is not possible in the political realm, however, until we have a new context in which to see our possibilities and an idea of where we are leading ourselves. To lead means we are going somewhere. Without this new awareness, we cannot lead, but only maintain or improve the status quo — whether on the right, left, or center.

When we understand our evolutionary potential, however, and awaken to our emerging social, spiritual, and scientific capacities to fulfill an evolutionary agenda, new political leadership will cocreate and consciously choose the meme needed to empower it. Society will be activated with excitement and hope as creative possibilities call forth the potential of millions.

The meme of profit-centered, self-centered capitalism also fails as a worldview to guide us into the 21st century. We see the spread of poverty, damage to the environment, and massive power in the hands of ever fewer individuals and global corporations. Paul Hawken wrote in *The Ecology of Commerce,*

> Like a sunset effect, the glories of industrial capitalism may mask the fact that it is poised at a declining horizon of options and possibilities. Just as internal contradictions brought down the Marxist and socialist economies, so do a different set of social and biological forces signal our own possible demise.[8]

The current economic system is not sustainable. According to Hawken, we are involved in a slow motion holocaust to our life-support system. If we do not recognize that every business, corporation, or enterprise is part of the whole system, and must take feedback from the whole system, and be accountable for its effect on the environment, we cannot continue to evolve, or even survive. Billionaire financier George Soros wrote in the *Atlantic Monthly*, February 1997,

> Although I have made a fortune in the financial markets, I now fear that the untrammeled intensification of laissez-faire capitalism and the spread of market values into all areas of life is endangering our open and democratic society. The main enemy of the open society, I believe, is no longer the communist but the capitalist threat.[9]

The Importance of Memes

In the past, memes arose unconsciously and directed our actions, often without our knowing consent. But now, not only are we responsible for our actions, but we are also responsible for our beliefs. For as we see reality, so we act, and as we act, so we shape reality. All ideas are human made, and none are the absolute truth. Common sense dictates that we evaluate our beliefs on the basis of how they affect us. If they make us more loving, creative, and wise, they are good beliefs. If they make us cruel, jealous, depressed, and sick, they cannot be good beliefs or memes.

For example, I tried in my early years to be what I thought was an existentialist. It was in Paris before I met my husband. I smoked Gauloises, drank red wine, and tried to believe in the meaninglessness of the universe and of myself. I became more despairing. Later, in the 1950s when my husband and I went to parties in New York, I occasionally expressed a naive sense of hope — that something magnificent was to come from human enterprise. The artists, poets, and playwrights of that time, imbued with an existentialist, or even a nihilistic, worldview scorned me and sent me home in tears! I became determined to find out what I was hopeful about! I searched through literature seeking clues to discover a new image of humanity, a new meme that not only seemed true, but was also scientifically sound and would correspond with my intuitive sense of meaning and hope. As I discovered the ideas of such evolutionary thinkers as Teilhard de Chardin, Abraham H. Maslow, Buckminster Fuller, Lancelot Law Whyte, Margaret Mead, Ruth Benedict, and Jonas Salk, my beliefs changed and my life transformed.

I was exhilarated and motivated to seek my vocation in the world. I wrote and published the "Center Letter," a first networking letter to more than 1,000 leaders at the frontier of change, asking them what they thought was the next step for the future good. I called people I admired, like Maslow, and invited them to lunch. Maslow gave me 300 names of his "Eupsychian network" to write to.

I will never forget the day I met Jonas Salk. I had written a letter to Jerry Piel, president of *Scientific American* magazine, describing my ideas of a "theater of man," which I heard Jonas wanted to build at the newly forming Salk Institute. Jonas read the letter, called me, and said we were "two peas in the same evolutionary pod." In September 1964 he invited me to lunch. He was the first truly evolutionary soul I encountered. Conscious evolution was the theme of his life. I shared with him all the ideas I had gleaned from my reading and then told him what was "wrong" with me — my love of the future and my desire to connect with everything. He smiled and said, "Barbara, these are not faults, these are exactly the characteristics needed by evolution. You are a mutant." (This was the first I had heard of what we are now calling imaginal cells.) Jonas introduced me to others who shared my perspective. I met Louis Kahn, the architect who was building the Salk Institute; Al Rosenfeld, science editor of *Life* magazine; and others. Suddenly this strange and somewhat lost person grew into a highly motivated futurist and social innovator. I wrote in my journal, Christmas 1964,

> ... the problem of identity has disappeared. I can never again say, as I once did, "in my own eyes I am nothing," for as all people are, I too am the inheritor of the evolution of the ages. In my genes are the generations. Every cell in my body identifies me with the great and terrible adventure of inanimate to animate to human, and every desire of my being sets me passionately to work to further the rise of humaneness out of humanity. I am what was and what will be. If I am nothing, life is nothing; that it cannot be — and be.[10]

Through the ideas and the affirmation of kindred souls, all imbued with the new meme of conscious evolution, my life transformed and I set upon the ever-evolving evolutionary journey. The new meme made all the difference.

Alfred Korzybski, whose work helped found the field of general semantics, made the point that the map is not the territory in his seminal book, *Science and Sanity*.[10] The word is not the thing just as the belief about reality is not reality itself. We become conscious that we are abstracting from a vast nonverbal event through our nervous systems. This abstraction reaches our brains and becomes meaningful to us through our personal worldview — through the image of reality that we hold. People with different pictures of reality see events differently and therefore act differently. Our worldview is important. It profoundly shapes how we see reality and how we act.

As David L. Cooperrider writes in *Appreciative Management and Leadership: The Power of Positive Thought and Action in Organizations*,

> to a far greater extent than is normally acknowledged, we human beings create our own realities through symbolic and mental processes and that because of this conscious evolution of the future is a human option.[12]

I can think of no finer lens to see the world through than conscious evolution. It expands our horizon to see humanity moving toward a higher dimension of life itself. I believe that conscious evolution is the emerging meme needed to guide us toward a more just, humane, and regenerative world.

The effort to develop a new meme is a vital aspect of feeding the hungry, healing the sick, stopping the violence, and freeing the world of poisonous toxins. The most direct path to our survival and fulfillment is to develop and communicate an idea system that guides us toward ethical evolution.

CHAPTER EIGHT

Embracing Conscious Evolution

As we have seen, conscious evolution is a "mother" meme calling together individual memes that hold information for creating new communications, arts, sciences, education, business, environmental organizations, and health systems — the new social body. Conscious evolution encourages all groups to come together and compose a great and magnificent matrix in which to flourish — a new memetic code for the emerging social body. Our mother meme provides a magnetic field for this momentous gathering. We might call our new memetic code the chrysalis in which the butterfly self-assembles.

The Fulfillment of Human Endeavor

Conscious evolution calls upon scientists and technologists to help us understand the laws and recurring patterns in the evolutionary process. This understanding will guide us in designing and using new technologies for our evolutionary agenda, the ethical evolution of ourselves toward universal life — the next turn in the evolutionary spiral.

Conscious evolution calls upon political leaders to move us toward a synergistic democracy that considers each of us as creative members of the whole community and ecology. We need to be guided toward the next stage of individualism. The success of modern society has led to new problems: the separation of individuals from one another, from their families, from their communities, and now from their jobs, as corporations downsize and all allegiances dissolve in the quest for survival and concern for the bottom line. Conscious evolution sets the stage for the next phase of individualism wherein we seek our uniqueness not through separation but through deeper participation in the whole.

Conscious evolution needs evolutionary artists to tell the story in a variety of ways. Currently we are in the catacombs, like early Christians, scratching pictures on the walls of caves as we communicate through journals, conferences, lectures, seminars, books, and tapes. Where are the vibrant and popular images — theater, music, dance, novels, poetry, films; where are the participatory art forms that inspire and lift our vision to help us see ourselves as participants in the great human drama of creation? Evolutionary artists are needed to bring our new story of creation to life, much like the great Greek playwrights, sculptors, and architects did for the Homeric stories and the genius of the Middle Ages did to illuminate the Gospels. The new arts of the age of conscious evolution will help us see ourselves anew — in all our hidden beauty as young universal humans.

Conscious evolution calls upon humanistic, transpersonal, and spiritual psychologies to move us from the early phase of personal growth and self-empowerment to the later stages of self-realization and self-transcendence as cocreators. Evolutionary psychology is needed to help us nurture within ourselves our higher qualities, to become mature, sovereign, cocreative humans attuning to the patterns of creation.

Conscious evolution calls for educators to design a metadiscipline, a new educational system in which teachers and students join together and create a new intellectual basis for transformative education. Such a basis would lead us from the confusion of the modern world to the fulfillment of the evolutionary agenda — freeing ourselves from hunger, disease, ignorance, and war — and to the release of human creativity and the universal future awaiting us. We need educators to help our children understand that they are a treasure and that education is a treasure hunt to help them find their unique genius, which can then be used where it is most needed in the world.

Conscious evolution calls upon the military genius to help us learn how to shift from weaponry to "livingry," as Buckminster Fuller poetically declared. We need to reorient our extraordinary organizational and technical capacities to restore our environment, protect us from natural disasters and terrorists, and develop peace-building and conflict resolution skills while we explore and develop our extended environment in outer space.

Conscious evolution calls on businesses and entrepreneurs to apply their genius to the development of socially responsible business and investment. The goal is a sustainable, regenerative economy that supports restoration of the environment, preservation of species, and the enhancement of human creativity and community, including expanded ownership, network marketing, community-based currencies, microcredit loans, and other such innovations.

Conscious evolution is the context for a "meta-religio," a new ground of the whole, calling upon spiritual leaders and practitioners of all faiths to create what Bishop William Swing, Episcopal bishop of California, calls a "United Religions" to end the conflict among religions and to bring together the unique gifts of the faiths for the future of humanity. We need to move beyond ecumenical understanding to evolutionary fulfillment through the embodiment of the principles and practices of the great faiths. We long not for a new religion, but for the evolution of religion, such that we embody the qualities of our master teachers and become conscious cocreators with the divine universal intelligence ourselves.

My friend Sidney Lanier has written stirring words for the soul in his personal journal,

> Conscious evolution is a meta-religio for the 21st century. As yet it is undefined and casts an evocative shadow over the mental inscape of all of us in these days. We know something is over: an era or simply the nightmare that has terrified many of us into awareness, simple human maturity. This meta-religio is the head-long convergence of science with the core realizations of the major world religions. Its constituency is the universal sovereign persons — awakened ones — all those who stand free of the old divisive social forms, however noble their past history. We are called to come together in an open and level place with no boundaries, a space in consciousness where we are enfolded within the transcendent community of the universal person, the sacred precincts of the cosmos itself, our temple and home.[1]

Innovators and creators in these and many more fields of human endeavor and thought are already creating vital new memes and are taking action based on these new ideas. When we piece together the picture of what is already happening, we will see the design emerge — the awakening of the social potential movement.

The Mystery of Evolution

The mystery of the process of creation is profound. Whether one believes that the process occurs through basic laws of natural selection and random mutation or one sees a divine design guiding the process — mind in the cosmos, God in the form of deity or an eternal animating force — the mystery is equally great. Whatever our beliefs, whatever our metaphysical preferences, we are all confronted with a sense of awe and reverence at the exquisite balance of nature, the precise workings of biological organisms, the wonder of the billions of galaxies and the equally infinite fields of subatomic physics where matter disappears and only probabilities exist in a vacuum that may indeed hold the memory of the whole process of creation. Within this mystery I have perceived some insights that must evolve as understanding grows:

• A designing, creative intelligence animates the universe. It is symbolized by the core running through the evolutionary spiral. As we mature on a personal and spiritual level, this intelligence becomes personal and conscious through us. God, the creative force of the universe, becomes person as us, yet is never subsumed or limited by us. When we look at the intelligence of the whole system — the design of every atom, molecule, and cell — there appears to be something more at work than can be attributed to particles alone. The assumption here is that there is a system of consciousness that transcends its parts, is immanent within them, yet is more than those parts.

The hypothesis out of which conscious evolution arises is that there exists a universal intelligence that informs the entire evolutionary process — a process that resides in part within the human psyche. In conscious evolution humanity remembers its past as well as its potential future, just as the genetic code of a biological organism holds the memory of its past and provides the design for its potential, yet not predetermined future. As Prof. A. Harris Stone wrote in a personal correspondence, "Conscious evolution can be seen as an awakening of the 'memory' that resides in a synthesis of human knowing — spiritual, social, and scientific — joined in the effort to discover the inherent evolutionary design, a design which we strive to manifest through ethical choice and creative action." [2]

• There is both an eternal and an evolving aspect of reality. The eternal is the nonphysical, nonlocal, ineffable "field of all possibilities," as Deepak Chopra called it in his book *The Seven Spiritual Laws of Success*.[3] It is pure consciousness experienced by us subjectively in nondual union with Source or Spirit through meditation, yoga, and other spiritual or mystical experiences.

The evolving aspect of the transcendent occurs when the unmanifest manifests in form. It resides in the implicate order. The timeless unfolds as duration. In evolution, the One becomes the many. Yet in each of the many resides the One. Each of us reflects both the eternal and the evolving aspects of the universal intelligence. Mystical experience of the past emphasized the eternal aspect of reality. As we enter the age of conscious evolution, however, we become more sensitive to the evolving aspect. We feel it as our motivation to grow, to know, to cocreate a new world commensurate with our aspirations for peace, love, and union with Source.

• We are an integral part of the evolutionary journey. In our genes are all generations of experience. In our genius is the code of conscious evolution. In our awakening lies the patterns of the planetary transition from our current phase to the next phase. Our mind is designed to know the design of evolution toward higher consciousness and freedom.

• This evolutionary process has a tendency toward higher consciousness and freedom through more complex or synergistic order, a tendency that is operative in us and can be accessed spiritually, socially, and scientifically. We are capable of resonating and cooperating with the tendency to fulfill our own greater potential and that of society as a whole.

• The universe is unitive, consistent throughout. There is one animating spiritual intelligence with infinitely diverse expressions of itself. Each of us is a living manifestation of that intelligence — sacred, unique, precious, and vital to the evolution of the whole.

Based on these assumptions, conscious evolution provides us a natural value system as we observe the recurring patterns of evolution. We learn to value and work deliberately to cultivate greater consciousness and freedom through more complex and harmonious order. It gives us an internal relatedness to the cosmos and to all Earth life as members of one body. It provides us with an eschatology — a sense of end times, which for us is not the end of the world but rather the beginning of the new as we make our shift from human to cocreative human.

It offers us a teleology, a sense of purpose and design in natural phenomena, that of becoming ever more cocreative with the universal tendency toward higher life. It offers a synthesis of *telos*, the study of ends, of final purposes, and *eros*, passionate love. In conscious evolution we become "telerotic" — in love with the fulfillment of the potential of the whole.

Conscious evolution provides an entelechy — a sense of ourselves when fully realized rather than merely potential. It is that still-undefined term cocreator or universal human that we have seen manifested in great beings such as Buddha and Jesus, which is now coming to fruition in us. We recognize our growth motivation as the vital force of evolution urging us toward self-fulfillment and wholeness.

Conscious evolution gives us a context and logic for the emergence of the social potential movement. We are not working in a dying or meaningless universe. We are working in alignment with the whole process of creation. This process has a direction that is animating our heart's desire for greater freedom, union, and transcendence. The new meme encourages each of us to attune to our own creative urge, to express our potential for the sake of ourselves and the world. It urges us to find others and cocreate together. It gives meaning to the present as the fruition of evolution, the moment in which the wisdom of the entire past comes to life in the expression of each individual cocreator. Conscious evolution offers us the possibility of an open-ended, choiceful, glorious future. Within each of us stirs the mighty force of creation in the process of its next quantum transformation.

PART III

THE SOCIAL POTENTIAL MOVEMENT

CHAPTER NINE

From the Human Potential to the Social Potential Movement

The social potential movement is the societal expression of conscious evolution. It has been latent throughout history because there has always been a longing in the human heart for a more just, free, loving, and creative society. But it was never before possible to fulfill these aspirations, because we had neither the evolutionary drivers and global crises to force us to change, nor did we have the scientific and technological powers that can free us from the limitations of scarcity, poverty, disease, and ignorance. This is the time of awakening for the social potential movement.

The social potential movement identifies peaks of social creativity and works toward social wellness and transformation, just as the human potential movement identifies peak experiences in our personal lives and cultivates individual wellness and transformation. The movement seeks out innovations now working in health, environment, communication, education, government, economics, technology, and other fields of human endeavor while designing new social systems that lead toward a regenerative and life-enhancing global society.

Our aspirations for a society in which all people are free to be and do their best can now be fulfilled. We are speaking here of metamorphosis — the natural emergence of the societal butterfly.

Dee Ward Hock, the founder of Visa, said,

> We are at that very point in time when a 400-year old age is dying and another is struggling to be born — a shifting of culture, science, society, and institutions enormously greater than the world has ever experienced. Ahead, the possibility of the regeneration of individuality, liberty, community, and ethics such as the world has never known, and a harmony with nature, with one another, and with the divine intelligence such as the world has never dreamed.[1]

The Path of the Cocreator

The foundation of the social potential movement is the emergence of the cocreative person, which has been the work of the human potential movement. We have been preparing for this path for thousands of years, through the great religious and ethical traditions, as previously mentioned. Yet only in our generation have we gained the actual powers of cocreation — the ability to become an integral part of the creative processes of nature and evolution.

In traditional religious language, we were created in the image of God and are becoming ever more godlike. In evolutionary language, we were created by the process of evolution and are becoming coevolutionary with that process. In cocreation we bring forth two strands — our spiritual essence and our scientific and social capacities — to participate in the creation. When these strands blend, a new human is born: a universal human, a cocreator, a unique and personal expression of the divine.

The most fundamental step on the path of the cocreator is a new spirituality in which we shift our relationship with the creative process from creature to cocreator — from unconscious to conscious evolution. Through resonance with the metapattern that connects us all, we learn to take responsibility for our part in the creation of our own evolution.

Building on the story of the Western world, the spiritual path of the cocreator dawns on the eighth day of creation. In Genesis, God is said to have finished the work of the creation on the seventh day, rested, and saw that it was good. On the *eighth* day of creation, however, we are waking up to find that we are responsible for the creation. To fulfill this responsibility, we must gain an ever greater resonance with the process of creation, or in traditional terms, with the will of God. We are speaking here of nothing less than the spiritual maturation of humanity.

Out of this emerging cocreative spirituality comes the cocreative person. The cocreative person is one who is motivated by Spirit, awakened in the heart, and activated to express unique creativity for the sake of the self and the world. Although such persons have existed occasionally throughout history never before has the genius within masses of us been called forth and expressed. The cocreative person is a new archetype on Earth. Our emergence is signaled by the shift from maximum procreation to cocreation. This archetype has emerged during the period of our birth, when Earth has reached her population limits. As we have fewer children and live longer lives with greater awareness, opportunity, and mobility, the cocreative person is appearing by the millions. They are imaginal cells, cultural creatives proliferating in the body of the social caterpillar.

The loving energy that went into self reproduction is now available for self evolution. This energy seeks to express life purpose. Just as we each have a genetic code, we also have a genius code — our individual creativity, the creator-within, now awakening and deeply desirous of expression in the world. Our spirituality is coming forth in spirit-motivated creative action.

The cocreative person is born when we experience an inner calling and say yes to that calling. In cocreation we are saying yes to the birth of our full potential self — that we will go the whole way in identifying our life purpose and bringing it forth as best we can into the world. This is as great a commitment as the birth and nurturance of a newborn child. In *Building Your Field of Dreams*, Rev. Mary Manin Morrissey detailed the precise steps needed to realize our inner callings in action.[2] We proceed not by default of birth, geography, class, or background, but by the voluntary commitment to evolve ourselves and serve the human community.

As we become cocreative persons, our intimate relationships change. We are no longer primarily the procreative couple. Men and women join now, not only to have a child, but also to help give birth to each other, to support each other in full self-expression. As the old family structure breaks up, the new cocreative family emerges, based not only on the joining of our genes to have a child, but also on the joining of our genius, to give rise to our full, creative selves.

Finally, many of us are experiencing vocational arousal, the wild and exciting desire to find our calling and express it in meaningful work. The drive to cocreate is rising as the need for maximum procreation declines. But, society does not yet have the social or economic systems in place to nurture and support the expression of this untapped creativity. Establishing new systems that can call forth our best is the work of the social potential movement. A sea of creativity is welling up from within us, which can evolve our world. It is this creativity that new social innovations seek to release. Through new forms of education, new economic systems, participatory management, and team-building and learning organizations, the social potential movement will learn how to channel this loving and creative energy for the social good.

The Convergence of Awareness and Action

Our personal growth has set the stage for the awakening of the social potential movement. It is relatively easy to evolve ourselves and our intimate relationships in family and at work. But what about the larger world? We look outside ourselves and we see social chaos, degradation, and overwhelming, complex problems — environmental degradation, overpopulation, resource depletion, hunger, poverty, social injustice, and alienation. To many, it seems impossible to solve these problems. We just do not have the time or the resources to coordinate a planetary economic and ecological system as rapidly as seems to be necessary to sustain and renew our threatened life-support systems. Some observers claim we have but a few decades to change our behavior in order to survive.

If we are really at this threshold of evolution or extinction, as Ervin Laszlo suggested, what could naturally facilitate this shift in time to save our world from the tragedies of environmental collapse or further social misery, hunger, poverty, and pain?

I believe there are two critical elements that can ease our transition and bring new hope for our fulfillment in the Third Millennium. One is the mass alignment of the consciousness that is already shifting toward a more unitive stage.

Creating events that align the consciousness of those already shifting toward a more cosmic, unitive form of awareness is vital.

By reinforcing our higher consciousnesses through resonance with others, we are infusing what Rupert Sheldrake called the "morphogenetic field," as described earlier, and are making unitive consciousness more accessible to all people. These events are initiated whenever two or more kindred souls come together to reinforce each other's emergent qualities of being.

As we approach the Third Millennium, however, we need vast celebrations that can catalyze a critical mass of people to experience a sense of oneness, empathy toward one another, and relatedness as members of one global family: a great awakening. Many millennial events are now in preparation for just such an awakening. (See Part 5: A Call To Action for millennium websites.)

Continuing with the birth analogy, we might expect that a planet is naturally ready for its collective awakening shortly after its period of birth, just as a biological organism becomes aware of itself soon after its birth. We are at that precise time of awakening in our planetary life cycle. Therefore, it may take only a relatively small effort to catalyze this shared awakening.

Another vital element is to find a way to accelerate connections among innovations currently working to change the world so that untapped creativity is channeled into meaningful work that expresses the individual's unique creativity.

An increased alignment of unitive consciousness combined with increased interaction among creative innovations is critical to a more gentle transition to the next stage of our evolution. The good news is that both elements are possible and, in fact, are beginning to happen. What we are suggesting here is a small nudge in the direction of greater convergence of the positive.

Nature's Secret Revealed

Is the convergence of our higher consciousness and expanded creativity enough to tip the scales in favor of a positive future, given the rapid escalation of problems that threaten our survival? I believe the answer is yes, because it is the nature of nature to repattern itself quickly when in conditions of extreme instability, such as we are experiencing through our environmental crisis. Although there are no certainties — we are potentialists, not optimists or pessimists — we can find a logical basis for pragmatic hope in the fabulous, unimaginable 15-billion-year journey of transformation. Our new story of creation has revealed to us five lessons of evolution. We have seen that:

- quantum transformations are nature's tradition;
- crises precede transformation;
- holism is inherent in the nature of reality;
- evolution creates beauty, and everything that endures is beautiful;
- evolution raises consciousness and freedom through more complex order.

These recurring patterns give us a basis for hope. Yet, to actually cooperate with nature, to align ourselves with the patterns of creation, we must know something more of how nature evolves. Our question must now be, How did nature rise from subatomic particles to you and me?

Does nature's capacity to take quantum jumps, to create more complex whole systems with ever greater capacity, give us any hints as to how we may consciously guide our evolution? I believed the answer was waiting for us, hidden in nature's 15 billion years of experience. Yet I searched for years to find the missing link that could help us get across the abyss from one quantum jump to the next.

I discovered a vital clue in *The New York Times* on October 12, 1977. That single article was tremendously helpful in my search for understanding how we could make a quantum jump from our current social crises to an immeasurable future. The headline read "A Chemist Told How Life Could Defy Physics Laws."[3] The physicist was Nobel-prize winner Ilya Prigogine (pronounced *prig*-a-gene). He discovered the process whereby life evolves into more complex systems given the Second Law of Thermodynamics. This law states that in a closed system energy inevitably increases in entropy or disorder. Based on this "fatal" law, scientists have predicted that the universe will inevitably end in a "heat death" — the degradation of all matter and energy in the universe to an ultimate state of inert uniformity. In other words, all the stars in the billions of galaxies will burn out and destroy their planetary systems. Life as we know it is but a momentary use of this dying energy and will be destroyed with no hope for life to continue in a universe so structured that it inevitably dies. This law formed the scientific basis of much of modern pessimism.

The questions become: How, then, has life increased in "negentropy," or order, for billions of years? How, in the face of this inevitable tendency for the universe to increase in disorder, has more complex order increased for billions of years and is presumably still increasing? What are the mechanisms whereby higher order is achieved in nature? And, how might we learn from this process to facilitate our own leap to higher order — toward greater freedom, love, awareness, spirituality, and the proper use of tangible and intangible resources the universe has provided for us?

Prigogine found a clue in his theory of dissipative structures. A dissipative structure is an open system in nature whose form, or structure, is maintained by a continuous dissipation, or consumption of energy. All living systems are dissipative structures — including humans. In *The Aquarian Conspiracy*, Marilyn Ferguson described how "living things have been running uphill in a universe that is supposed to be running down."

Ferguson continued in her discussion of Prigogine,

> The continuous movement of energy through the system results in fluctuations; if they are minor, the system damps them and they do not alter its structural integrity. But if the fluctuations reach a critical size, they perturb the system. They increase the number of novel interactions within it.... The elements of the old pattern come into contact with each other in new ways and make new connections. The parts reorganize into a new whole. The system escapes into a higher order. As Prigogine said, at higher levels of complexity, the nature of the laws of nature changes. Life feeds on entropy. It has the potential to create new forms by allowing a shake-up of old forms. The elements of a dissipative structure cooperate to bring about this transformation of the whole.[4]

When I read this, I felt like a detective searching to understand how society could make a quantum jump from our current crises to a future equal to our new powers. We cannot get there by linear, incremental steps alone, given the world's accumulating crises. But the process of transformation is not linear! Systems become more complex by nonlinear, exponentially increasing numbers of interactions of incremental innovations. At some point apparently insignificant innovations connect in a nonlinear manner. Everything that rises converges and connects, becomes synergistic and cocreative. The system then cooperates in its own self-transcendence in an apparent sudden shift. This shift has been building for a long time out of myriad innovations silently and invisibly interacting and connecting beneath the surface of our attention — the work of early imaginal cells in the body of the disintegrating caterpillar.

SOCIAL TRANSFORMATION MODEL

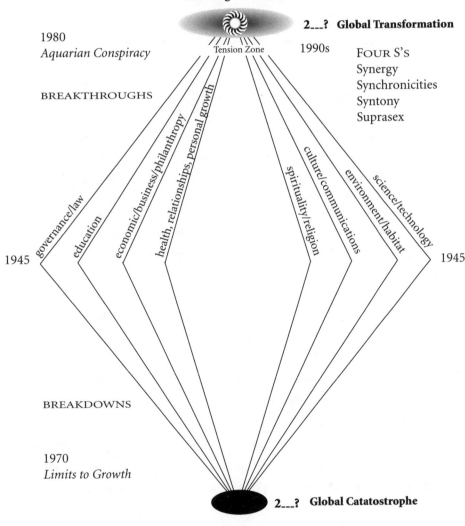

Convergence Zone

2___? **Global Transformation**

1980
Aquarian Conspiracy

Tension Zone   1990s

FOUR S'S
Synergy
Synchronicities
Syntony
Suprasex

BREAKTHROUGHS

governance/law
education
economic/business/philanthropy
health, relationships, personal growth
spirituality/religion
culture/communications
environment/habitat
science/technology

1945   1945

BREAKDOWNS

1970
Limits to Growth

2___? **Global Catatostrophe**

Let's apply the Prigogine model to our personal and social evolution. If nature has been working through dissipative structures for billions of years, the same process must be working through us now. We can better facilitate the natural and ease all our transitions when we understand the process.

Human society is a large dissipative structure that is increasingly perturbed and is undergoing fluctuations. In our communities, systems are increasingly unstable or dysfunctional. We are using more of our energy to handle these problems in ways that seem ineffective, like building more weapons and prisons for greater security or fighting a war against drugs when kids roam aimlessly in the streets with nothing to do and nowhere to go. Hunger, poverty, social and economic injustice, violence in our communities and schools, resource depletion, pollution, overpopulation, the loss of rain forests, toxic wastes — all are escalating and all tend to converge in catastrophe.

Meanwhile, social innovations, or "improved mutations," are springing up everywhere. Thousands of acts of caring, sharing, healing, and new solutions are emerging. Applying the model of dissipative structures to our situation, we see that social innovations that share a similar value system are converging, connecting, and networking at an increasing rate. This process is accelerating rapidly through the Internet. However, will the convergence of positive innovations happen before the convergence of destructive tendencies? Will the planetary system repattern to a higher order, or will it fall apart into chaos, into environmental collapse that has also been predicted? This is the question. There is no guarantee that a dissipative structure will repattern to a higher order. It is merely a tendency, just as it is the tendency of each baby to survive, although many do not.

It is precisely at this point that we need a new social innovation to facilitate the increased interaction among positive innovations — a new ground of the whole to facilitate this convergence.

This *is* the first age of conscious evolution. We must enter the process of our own evolution consciously. How can we do this? We can set in motion a new social function to hasten the nonlinear interaction of positive social innovations and to facilitate the natural repatterning of our society to a more harmonious order, thus saving ourselves from the predicted catastrophes.

CHAPTER TEN

Testing the Waters

After I discovered a clue, with the help of the Prigogine model, as to how nature evolves, I wanted to find a way to test my discovery in the real world. I had moved to Washington D.C. in 1970 and later cofounded The Committee for the Future, an organization whose purpose was to bring positive options for the future into the public arena for discussion and action. I was connected with innovators and potentialists throughout the country. As we were approaching 1984 — known as the Year of the Woman — I decided to do an experiment in conscious evolution by bringing the ideas of Abraham Maslow, Teilhard de Chardin, Buckminster Fuller, and many other new paradigm thinkers into the political arena. I became an "idea candidate" for the future of humanity, offering a new social function to accelerate the interaction of positive innovations and help the system repattern itself without further violence, suffering, or environmental degradation.

I formed the Campaign for a Positive Future and told all my friends and colleagues that I was in the running for selection as the Democratic vice-presidential candidate. (To be chosen by whomever was nominated for president as his vice presidential candidate.) I asked them to arrange opportunities for me to speak in order to gain support for my ideas. Many were delighted. Meetings were arranged, and I set out upon the most fascinating journey of my life.

A Campaign for What Works

To launch the campaign I created a new social function called the Office for the Future, or Peace Room (I used the two names interchangeably). This function would develop the idea of converging social innovations at the highest level of power. It was to reside in the office of the vice-president of the United States (which, I believe, is still an underdeveloped office). Under the direction of the vice-president, the Office for the Future was to become as sophisticated as a war room. In our war rooms we track enemies and strategize how to defeat them, so in our peace rooms we identify, connect, and communicate our successes, breakthroughs, and models that work. (Peace, in this context, is not defined as conflict resolution. It means peace through cocreation, through the full expression of human creativity in cooperation with nature, with one another, and with the deeper design of evolution.)

I proposed that the Office for the Future should have four functions that would facilitate the repatterning of our society to a higher order of consciousness, freedom, and synergistic order.

1. The office would scan for breakthroughs in all fields — health, education, media, science, government, business, the arts, community — wherever a person or small group invents or discovers something that creates a more life-enhancing world. Small acts

to great projects would be noted. It would invite citizens at the local level to form centers to scan their communities for creative innovations; our ambassadors would be asked to establish Peace Rooms to discover what works in their countries. (I did not realize at the time that what was missing was the new Internet technology.) I imagined that the world would be involved in discovering what is working. Can you imagine asking, "What's working in Iran, in Libya, in Yugoslavia?" David L. Cooperrider said,

> The more an organization [or any group or nation] experiments with the conscious evolution of positive imagery, the better it will become. There is an observable self-reinforcing, educative effect of affirmation. Affirmative competence is the key to the self-organizing system.[1]

2. The office would map these innovations according to function and geography to discover the pattern and design of what works. The anatomy of the social body would emerge. For example, in the area of education, all projects working on specific aspects of education, such as gifted children, lifelong learning, emotional maturity, and so forth, would be clustered in organic patterns until we could actually see the anatomy of what is working in each precise function of the social body. Soon we would have a picture of the emerging world. We envisioned large maps and graphs in the White House of progress toward the evolutionary agenda — the hierarchy of social needs — with constant input based on what the people are doing that works.

As a part of the official United States Bicentennial Celebration in 1976, the Committee for the Future had organized a synergistic convergence conference called SYNCON in Washington D.C. with futurist Alvin Toffler, author of *Future Shock* and *The Third Wave*.[2] We graphically presented the hierarchy of social needs on a huge chart. People were calling in from all over the country with their social innovations, which were placed on the chart where they belonged as they contributed toward meeting an aspect of the evolutionary agenda (meeting basic, growth, and transcendent need levels). We saw how the whole social system was evolving in a coherent way. The apparent chaos of social change became coherent when the separate items were placed where they fit best in the hierarchy of social needs. We saw the social body as a living system in transition from one stage of its evolution to the next, evolving through the myriad acts that countless unrelated individuals were doing. I used the metaphor of the Rose Window at Chartres Cathedral. Each pane of stained glass alone seems meaningless and insignificant, but when it becomes a part of the whole pattern of the Rose Window it is magnificent. Just so, each act alone may seem unimportant or random, but when allowed to self-organize as part of a living system, each act finds its natural place within the social body and is thereby seen to be a vital and even sacred part of the whole. Through this process we see the design of evolution, and each person can better find their unique place within the evolving system. The plan of action unfolds based on what is already working.

3. The office would connect people and projects for greater cooperation and effectiveness. It would be a powerful, upgraded networking function to help social innovators make vital connections needed with others. The deep human desire to relate, to connect, to join our genius is satisfied when we find our teammates and partners. Cocreation does not mean service at the sacrifice of self; it means service through the actualization of self. Self-actualization occurs when we find our vocations and express them meaningfully in the world. Our vocations are drawn forth by the process of finding others we need, by enlivening our individual lives and the quality of life in the community.

4. The office would communicate via all media the stories of the human family's successes and model projects. I suggested there be a weekly broadcast from the White House — "What Works in America" — calling for greater public participation, inviting people to join projects, to start new projects, to find their life purpose and come together to create the works and acts needed for the future of the human family. Volunteerism would come alive as the expression of our love and creativity in chosen work.

I sent out a "high fidelity bird call," as economist Hazel Henderson put it, and I got a certain kind of bird, all imaginal cells. Many had not been active in politics because, like myself, they had not thought they could make much of a difference. It was thrilling. Everywhere I went people said they wanted to form a center for it — whatever *it* is. *It* was not quite a political philosophy or a new party; *it* wasn't political at all, in the old sense of the word. I discovered that *it* was the center, the creative essence in each person awakened, amplified, connected, and manifested in creative action to serve some need in the community. People sought communion, community, and cocreativity, not something that any leader could do for them. *It* was what they could do for themselves by coming together in a new way. Yet, they found it exciting to have a political candidate support them in their initiatives.

Little centers sprung up everywhere, calling themselves Positive Future Centers. They were actually embryonic centers for cocreation. The people meditated and prayed; they worked on themselves and they reached into their communities, making their contributions to express their life purpose. Wherever I went I was at home. Even as a wife and mother raising my children, I had a strange longing for a deeper belonging. Now I had found it. Those little centers felt like home, a place for us to flock together, try our wings, and learn to fly. Each center was resonant with the evolutionary agenda and affirmed the new paradigm. People were interested in both the human and the social potential. They were eager to carry the inner work into the world. People sought to bring their love and creativity into the community, learning to repattern the larger world in the image of their higher selves.

Our goal was to model the change we wanted to see in the world. Only if we ourselves could evolve, could our society transform. "The best solution is our own conscious evolution," was one of our slogans. We began the work of politics from the inside out, on the personal level, while realizing that we needed systemic changes on the social scale.

I asked for leaders at the growing edge of every field to meet and discuss the options for a positive future. Buckminster Fuller was my mentor, along with Willis Harman, former president of the Institute of Noetic Sciences (founded by astronaut Edgar Mitchell to research the science of consciousness), family therapist Virginia Satir, and other outstanding innovators and creators of the new paradigm.

However, when the time came to attend the Democratic National Convention, politically sophisticated people told me, "Don't go to San Francisco, dear. You have done a good job at the grassroots level, but they will destroy you at a national convention." We had no money left, no media attention (we were told we were too positive), and no passes to the floor (the Democratic National Committee had ignored our campaign, telling us that the kind of person we were attracting was too self-centered to be of any value to them politically). Liberal political leaders felt that human potentialists were narcissistic and not to be taken into account, for in fact, we had not been active before. Traditional democrats focused on helping those oppressed and victimized, rather than empowering each other to free ourselves. Obviously both are needed, but we were the newer element, and had not yet found our voice. (Now there are at least the 44 million cultural creatives, many of whom are transformationally-motivated in the United States alone — a mighty force has arisen in the last 15 years.)

However impossible it seemed from any rational logic, ten of us decided to go to the convention, for my guidance was that we had not yet completed the mission of having my name placed in nomination for the vice-presidency. My purpose was to speak at the convention and call for the Office for the Future and the Peace Room, which would tell the story of humanity's evolutionary potential in a political context and plant the idea of the evolutionary agenda and a transformed presidency focused on what works.

Our task was to have 200 delegates sign a petition that would place my name in nomination so I could make my nominating speech before the convention, the nation, and the world. Doubt raged, for I had enough sense as a political science graduate to know that this was impossible. I should give up before suffering the humiliation of being totally ignored, for the chances of a grassroots, futuristic, unknown woman being nominated for the vice-presidency of the United States was less than zero. I was told we would be lucky to get one delegate, even if she were my mother!

We decided, however, to act as if we were going to succeed and to practice every metaphysical discipline any of us had learned. We arose at five every morning. We prayed; we loved one another; we forgave one another; we did creative visualizations of the nominating speech; we affirmed our victory with certainty; and, most important, we overcame doubt, using the technology of creating the future through structural tension. Our team continually chose and rechose our goal (no matter how impossible it seemed) while making friends with current reality — not denying anything about the truth of our situation. The tension between the goal and the current condition can snap one, like a taunt rubber band released, toward the goal. And it did.

We went into the hallways, the bars, the restaurants, and the early morning caucuses to sign up delegates. Occasionally I was given 30 seconds to speak at the caucuses. I was able to say, "My name is Barbara Marx Hubbard, I am running for the vice-presidency to propose an Office for the Future that will scan for, map, connect, and communicate positive innovations that work." The delegates signed up. And it wasn't just I that obtained the signatures. The ten people who formed the team — only one had been to a national convention — obtained most of the signatures. The resonance we had created among ourselves radiated and seemed to mesmerize the busy delegates. They really had no intention of nominating me for vice-president, but there was an *X factor*, a special appeal that attracted them to sign, almost against their better judgment. Many powerful political leaders were trying for this nomination, for it meant a televised speech before the world. We were up against a substantial field of well-known political leaders who were also attempting to obtain the 200 required signatures.

The first day we had 100 signatures. The second day we had another 100. On the third day, my campaign manager, Faye Beuby, took the petitions to the Democratic National Committee at the convention. We had more than 200 signatures. The Committee was horrified! Someone had gotten through the net. But to their credit they verified the petitions and authorized my nomination, although they moved up the convention two hours so that my speech would not get national prime time, only C-Span. Then the announcement came: two women's names were to be placed in nomination for the vice-presidency of the United States: Barbara Marx Hubbard and Geraldine Ferraro. I was stunned. It was a political paranormal experience! The impossible had happened.

I rushed to write the speech, *To Fulfill the Dream*, that we had been visualizing in so many church basements, living rooms, and small groups. When I was taken to the huge dais to speak, a guard led me to the microphone, holding my arm gently. "Honey," he said, "don't worry, they won't pay any attention to you, they never do...you're saying this for the universe." And so I did. I said, "The purpose of the United States of America is to emancipate the creativity of people everywhere." I expanded upon Thomas Jefferson, saying,

> We hold these truths to be self-evident;
> All people are born creative;
> Endowed by our Creator
> with the inalienable right and responsibility
> to express our creativity
> for the sake of ourselves and our world.

I proposed a choiceful future, a time when we would join together to meet basic needs, to restore the environment, to educate ourselves to realize our full potential and to explore the further reaches of the human spirit and our expanded environment in space. With all the power of my being I called for the new social function, the Peace Room, in the White House. The delegates were milling around, paying no attention, but as I spoke the words I realized for the first time the enormous power of focused action and faith. If a disorganized band of grass-roots environmentalists, businesspeople, housewives, futurists, and human potentialists could achieve this, imagine what we could do if we were well organized.

The Next Step

I learned from the campaign that the appeal of the new social function — to converge the positive — is almost irresistible. It was literally a political paranormal experience to have my name placed in nomination. It happened because the idea is obvious and intuitively almost all people want it to happen.

Secondly, I realized that in this campaign there were seeds of a new approach to politics that could work. Mine was a symbolic idea campaign, I am not a politician. I do not have organizing skills. I am a communicator of ideas and a stimulator of vision. From the campaign's modest, yet remarkable, success, however, I saw how a real team might succeed in transforming American politics, opening it up to a more participatory and creative democracy.

A presidential and vice-presidential team should form and select ahead of time members of a cabinet who know well the social innovations in their fields. The team would work together, discover, and link up with what is now working to create a positive future. After they have identified key innovations in each field, they would spend the needed time developing a platform based on the further development of what works. It is a design for a positive future. The presidential candidate would introduce the team the American people will actually be electing if they elect the candidate president. Each team member would speak briefly about what he or she knows really works for solving a problem. The team would then introduce major social innovators who briefly discuss the success of their projects. The vice-presidential candidate would promise to establish the Office for the Future in the White House.

The presidential team would invite people to tell them more of what works in each region of the country and ask them to form centers to continue to scan for, map, connect, and communicate breakthroughs in their communities. These campaign events would attract local media and elected officials. Efforts would be made to connect people and projects and to continually facilitate cocreation among people. The presidential team would become a magnet for the positive. Using the Internet, the team could not only connect and communicate the positive in this country, but could join with teams in other countries who choose to do the same for their societies. We would quickly cultivate a new movement for positive change rising throughout the world.

I believe that such a campaign would have a beneficent effect on the political process and would inspire candidates from all parties and at all levels of government to run on the people's innovation and creativity.

My sense is that the timing is right to take the next step in the manifestation of this vision. The Cold War is over. The insane threat of nuclear winter has receded. The fatalistic worldview caused by those ominous possibilities has largely dissolved, leaving people without a meme or vision to guide them. The desire for democracy is rising throughout the world. People are demanding the right to choose, both socially and personally. And people are increasingly aware of what is *not* working. Growing numbers are outraged by economic and social injustice affecting millions in the United States and billions throughout the world. Yet, solutions are also becoming better known through the expanding networking of organizations and groups, the astonishing growth of the Internet, and the growing interest in media that feature positive news.

Globalization is accelerating and having a major impact on our noosphere. It is empowering us to address en masse the seminal questions of the direction and values of society in the 21st century. In this increasingly memeless world, the new meme of conscious evolution would serve people seeking deeper direction and meaning in their lives.

In the past decades, the human potential movement has matured. People are learning a deep level of personal responsibility for their lives and are ready to reach into their communities. Our coconspirators, the cultural creatives, have emerged as the fastest growing subculture in the United States. They are gaining influence in all fields of endeavor. Furthermore, technological breakthroughs foster this movement, especially the Internet.

It may be that we are heading for a long boom or toward an environmental or economic collapse. No one knows. It depends on what we do personally and collectively. The social dissipative structure is in a highly nonequilibrium state. It can repattern itself toward breakdown and catastrophe or toward breakthrough and transformation. It is like a supersaturated solution ready to crystallize.

Since my campaign people have continually asked, "When is the Peace Room going to come into being?" In 1996 Nancy Carroll, the executive director of the Foundation for Conscious Evolution, along with Peter Russell, author of *The Global Brain Awakens*, began the process by putting an early version of the Peace Room on the Internet. Now, as the larger social potential movement gains momentum, we want to use the website to continue the story of social creativity in real time and discover what is now working. Our site is called "Cocreation" and serves as one of the catalysts for the development of a large-scale website as well as a mass media outreach. (See Part 5: A Call to Action for more information.)

CHAPTER ELEVEN

A Spirit-Motivated Plan
of Action for the 21st Century

From the perspective of the social potential movement, our goal for the 21st century should be a broad acceptance of the evolutionary agenda, supported by the worldview of conscious evolution and manifested through new social innovations and social systems that lead toward a positive and ever-evolving future. My vice-presidential campaign was an early initiative to bring this idea into the public arena. The key to its success was the pragmatic proposal to build the Peace Room. This was a metasocial innovation that could reinforce all innovations and facilitate the social dissipative structure to repattern itself to a higher order of complexity, consciousness, freedom, and capacity.

The Peace Room formed the basis of what organizational development specialist David Cooperrider called an appreciative inquiry,

> ...a process to seek out the best of "what is" to help ignite the collective imagination of "what might be." Its aim is to generate knowledge that expands the realm of the possible, helping us

envision a collectively desired future and carry forth that vision in ways that successfully translate images of possibility into reality.[1]

We might say poetically that we are aiming at a social lunar landing. In the 1960s John F. Kennedy proclaimed that "we would land a man on the moon and bring him back alive within the decade." What goal could we choose that, if achieved, would be a definitive change, a milestone for the social potential movement like the lunar landing was for the technologists?

I believe this goal should be to create and implement a new social function — the Peace Room — on a global scale within the first decade of the 21st century. This initiative will lead toward an expanded, democratic, and inclusive effort to facilitate the transition from one phase of evolution to the next. In every region of the world we would scan for, map, connect, and communicate what is working to create a humane, regenerative world — a cocreative society. Each nation and culture would strive to find its own way to empower its transformational leadership at the frontiers of positive change. In the United States, for example, by 2010 we might have a transformed American presidency that reflected and supported the values and structures of the social potential movement.

To achieve these goals we need a plan of action. During an Apollo mission, Dr. Thomas Paine, the NASA administrator at the time, showed me the flowchart that guided hundreds of thousands of separate tasks required for the lunar landing. I imagined at the time a planetary flow chart and a global Peace Room that would track the myriad initiatives in every field of endeavor, an indicative plan made up of everyone's plans so that we could all see what one another is doing, correct our own activities, and be more effective through collaboration.

PLANETARY FLOW CHART

Key Initiatives in Each Field
Self-mapped with time lines, goals, needs, and resources

	1998	1999	2000	2001	2002	2003	2004
Governance/Law							
Education							
Economics/ Business/ Philanthropy							
Health/ Relationships/ Personal Growth							
Environment/ Habitat							
Culture/Media/ Communications							
Spirituality/ Religion							
Science/ Technology							

This plan is obviously a huge task, far greater than a NASA project, if it is to be a Peace Room as sophisticated as a war room. We are speaking here of a vital social innovation to facilitate the shift in modern society from massive overemphasis on military and consumption to a cocreative, civil society based on the values now rising among cultural creatives throughout the world. I believe this is possible because the system is already shifting. We are only facilitating the natural interaction among innovating elements.

It will take many thousands of hours of research and diligence to establish the new function, and much more to maintain it over the years. The function will require a new taxonomy to establish the categories of social innovations, from individual and local to the global levels. It will also require the development of rigorous criteria and values, sophisticated information systems, knowledgeable networkers, holistic management, a brilliant business plan, and financial support — all of which are substantial. Yet, because this is a vital and necessary step, the question is not if this will happen; it is simply a matter of *when*.

Let's explore key steps needed to achieve this goal.

A New Social Architecture

One vital step is to develop a new model of society as a whole system in transition. When we view society now, we see it in its confused and apparently incoherent state. Social innovations are dispersed throughout the social body, often ignored, disconnected, and underfunded.

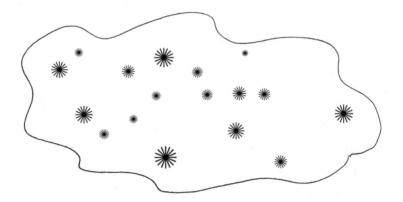

Now let's turn our evolutionary eye upon this social chaos.

This eye is a lens that sees from the evolutionary perspective. It holds within it the new meme of conscious evolution, and it has noticed that our society is a living organism in transition.

Let's look at our social body as a wheel divided into sectors that represent vital functions — health, education, environment, governance, and so on. Every system in the social body is currently under stress: environmental degradation, violence within communities, failing educational systems, and on and on. Yet, it is equally true that there are breakthroughs in every field and function. We do not consistently notice the breakthroughs, for we lack the evolutionary lens. When we view the current situation with our evolutionary eye, we see the implicit pattern of success in every functional area.

When we identify breakthroughs emerging whenever there are breakdowns, solutions whenever there are problems, we see the outlines of the emerging world. Each breakthrough or solution is a point of transformation created by innovators who are making something new work now. By connecting and communicating these innovations, we see elements of the design for a positive future in every field — not in the distant future, but as a pragmatic reality upon the frontiers of progress.

What We Mean By "What Works"

Along with the development of a model of the social body as a system in transition, we must deepen our inquiry into what we mean when we say that something works. This question is vital — for the way we respond to it will guide our selection of social innovations. Values form the fundamental basis of ethical evolution, which must be quickly learned if we are to use our new powers for life-oriented purposes. The question, "What do we mean by what works?" leads us to the very nature of the new society we choose to cocreate. Obviously, we don't mean a better gun or a faster car. Values must be considered by all of us throughout society. There can be no dogma here, only openness and tolerance of differences. As we seek the underlying metapattern that connects, the implicate order becomes explicate.

As a student of evolution, I suggest there are values inherent in the whole process of creation that can serve as guidelines to us now. These values — the fifth lesson of evolution — are higher consciousness and greater freedom through more complex or synergistic order. Evolution has moved in this direction with every quantum jump. By consciously working toward these values now, we are going with the process of creation, in alignment with a 15-billion-year trend.

From the evolutionary perspective, we value any act, intention, or belief that expands our consciousness toward a more unitive, spiritual, loving, whole-centered stage. We favor acts that support the ethics of all our religions to love one another, to "do unto others as we would have done unto ourselves," and to have reverence for higher dimensions of our own nature, for other species, and for Earth and the cosmos. Equally, we value acts that lead to greater freedom, both freedom from deficiencies of hunger, poverty, lack of self-esteem, and freedom to realize our untapped potential for self-actualization and chosen life purpose. Freedom without higher consciousness and the compassionate responsibility for others as well as ourselves can become self-centered and destructive. Yet, higher consciousness without freedom to act can become so inner directed that it cuts us off from social involvement, which is vital to the survival of humanity. This is the core reason why the social potential movement is so necessary now.

Finally, we select acts for the value of synergistic (win-win) order. This means we value whatever helps bring separate parts together into greater wholeness and cooperation — personally, in our intimate relationships, in our communities and among religions, nations, disciplines, races, and cultures. We value what joins us together to form a whole society that is different from, unpredictable from, and greater than the sum of its parts — the definition of synergy. The quest for shared values is intrinsic to the social potential movement.

The Innovations Wheel

The social body can be modeled in a variety of ways. An excellent wheel design has been developed over a 20-year period by Avon Mattison, president of Pathways to Peace, and many colleagues to demonstrate the dynamic — the evolutionary process of peace — in which the future is cocreated in harmony with one another, with nature, and with Spirit. Although it is named a Peace-Building Wheel©, in this context we call it the innovations wheel. Each of the eight sectors is a vital system of the whole, offering a visible matrix of the emerging social body in which we place our creative acts. The functional pattern is composed of countless separate innovations, as people place their initiatives in the wheel where they fit best. The wheel is the context for the mother meme described in a previous chapter, calling to her heart all precious memelets — ideas that hold the seed of the emerging civilization.

The following are eight sectors or pathways to social transformation — toward a peaceful, cocreative world. The guidelines and goals suggest some of the broad kinds of results we seek from the social innovations that are selected.

SECTORS	GUIDELINES AND GOALS
1. Governance and Law	• Participatory governing systems ensuring equity and justice for all • Rights and responsibilities • Empowerment of civil society • Security shifts from weaponry to livingry
2. Education	• Lifelong development of the whole person/whole planet • Free access to all systems of knowledge • Literacy • Leadership • Unfolding of innate wisdom
3. Economics, Business, Philanthropy	• Economic models that fairly and respectfully integrate all stakeholders • New community-based monetary systems, new value-based social indicators, expanded ownership, cooperative entrepreneurship, and socially responsible investing • Sustainable development, servant leadership
4. Health, Relationships, Personal Growth	• Harmonious interrelationship of the physical, emotional, mental, and soul levels

- Psychologies of growth
- Resolving conflicts within self and society
- Partnerships models of relationships

5. Science and Technology	• Scientific, technological, and noetic (mind) research for furthering the evolutionary success of life on Earth and in space
6. Spirituality and Religion	• Universal principles, ethics, and values • Practices of cocreation • Higher understanding of truth
7. Environment and Habitat	• Fulfilling basic human needs (food, water, shelter, etc.) and restoring the natural environment • Living systems and structures that integrate sustainable human needs with renewable material resources
8. Culture, Media, and Communications	• Building cultures of peace for succeeding generations • Life-enhancing arts, media, and communications

INNOVATIONS WHEEL WITH GOLDEN INNOVATIONS

Golden Innovations

The first function of the innovations wheel is to help identify what social analyst and activist Eleanor LeCain called golden innovations. A golden innovation is a project now working successfully that, if further developed and applied, could transform the system in which it functions. It differs from a simply good innovation in that it could have a quantum effect in addressing a major social ill.

Golden innovations are mutually reinforcing and interconnecting. They foster intrinsic values by embodying greater cooperation, creativity, optimism, a tolerance for differences, a sense of reverence for life, and faith in the potential of all people. They share an emphasis on self-actualization rather than on self-sacrifice. Ultimately, they form the basis of the cocreative society — the societal butterfly.

Criteria for golden innovations have been developed by Eleanor and Mark Donohue. The first three are subjective and qualitative. The others are quantitative and measurable.

1. The innovation moves society toward the goal of a just, humane, regenerative, and choiceful future — the evolutionary agenda.

2. It comprises core values of the new paradigm that embody higher consciousness, greater freedom, and more synergistic order. These values include integrity, sustainability, inclusivity, nonviolence, gender balance, and win-win solutions that foster freedom, personal responsibility, and respect for others and self.

3. It has the potential for major social impact; it is more than a good project, it is one that can assist in the positive transformation of a vital function in the social body.

4. Its success is measurable, and it has achieved better quantifiable results than the majority of other approaches in comparable fields of endeavor.

5. It is more cost effective than other approaches over the long term and ideally also in the short term.

6. It has at least a 2-year track record.

7. It is sustainable, replicable, and not dependent on one charismatic leader or other unique circumstances for its success.

Examples of golden innovations can be found in each sector of the wheel. Each embodies a story of dedication and love; each is a gift of creative action from heroes and heroines often unseen and unknown. These social entrepreneurs are people whose creativity and drive open major new possibilities in education, health, the environment, and other areas of human need. Just as business entrepreneurs lead innovation in commerce, social entrepreneurs drive social change.

What we need is a "search engine" to find peaks of social creativity. To set the scene for what is to come, I mention here but a few of the scores of social projects waiting to find their places within the process of transformation embodied in each sector of the wheel. (A useful reference is *The Book of Visions: An Encyclopedia of Social Inventions.*)[2]

In the field of education, for example, we can find innovations that reinforce the values of personal responsibility, freedom, and creativity. Eleanor LeCain reported in her forthcoming book, *What's Working in America,*

> Deborah Meier established several public schools in Harlem, New York, where teachers and students are excited about learning and 90 percent of students graduate and go on to college. Central Park East School achieves these results, even though the drop out rate in comparable schools for Black and Hispanic students is about 50 percent. In the realm of replicability of an innovation, Ms. Meier has moved to Boston and is reinventing her unique educational program in one of the city's worst areas, Mission Hill, while her colleagues have continued the success at Central Park East.[3]

A 1994 *Washington Post* story added, "As Gorbachev helped fracture the old Soviet Union, so Meier has led the movement to chop America's big high schools into vibrant little educational enclaves, many schools within a school."[4]

The Hunger Project, an international non-governmental organization (NGO) established in 1977 whose goal is the sustainable end of world hunger, is based on the same principle and focuses on the human component: empowering individuals to discover their own vision, express leadership, and work together to translate their vision into accomplishment. The Hunger Project does not provide food. It works on the principle of educating for self-reliance: empowering local people to create lasting solutions that enable them to gain access to health care, education, safe water, increased food production, better nutrition and incomes, and a more powerful, effective voice in the decisions that affect their lives. It gives top priority to empowering women. It has pioneered a new methodology, a dynamic people-centered, decentralized process known as Strategic Planning-in-Action, which has empowered people in India, Bangladesh, and Africa to achieve breakthroughs in health, education, food production, nutrition, and improved incomes. The Hunger Project mobilizes local leadership from all sectors and every level of society and empowers them to work together to achieve the end of hunger. Although hunger has not yet been overcome, wherever the Hunger Project is at work people are empowered. In this lies its success. Lynne Twist, who has raised more than $100 million for Hunger Project initiatives, says, "There is no such thing as a helpless person."

Building on this theme, in the area of crime prevention and rehabilitation the Delancy Street Project founded by Mimi Silbert in San Francisco takes hardened criminals and drug addicts whose lives are apparently hopeless, and through an intensive education in personal responsibility and caring for others transforms them into successful entrepreneurs with their own businesses, housing, and community. They take no government funds. The rate of recidivism is less than 10 percent — astonishingly low, versus a rate of approximately 50 percent for similar programs.

Ashoka is a world fellowship that provides the foundation for pattern-changing visionaries who are alone in the newness of their works. Ashoka's network helps these visionaries, called Fellows, to find and help each other by sharing their professional experiences and methodologies. Founded by William Drayton, Ashoka encourages and assists individuals in making important innovations for the public good and builds an active mutual help fellowship among such public service entrepreneurs, both established and beginning, across all barriers. For 15 years Ashoka has sought out and elected into its fellowship nearly 800 Fellows from Asia, Africa, Latin America, and Central Europe. The criteria for being selected to receive an Ashoka fellowship are the following:

- A New Idea: Does this person have a truly new idea for solving a public need?
- Creativity: Is he or she creative both in vision and goal setting and in problem solving?
- Entrepreneurial Quality: Is it impossible for this person to rest until his or her vision is the new pattern across society, even if it involves years of relentless grappling with myriad how-to issues?
- Social Impact of the Idea: Is the idea itself sufficiently new, practical, and useful so ordinary people will adopt it after it has been demonstrated? How many people will be affected by this idea? How important and how beneficially will they be affected?
- Ethical Fiber: If you were in danger, would you instinctively trust this person? Would you trust him or her in public office?

These criteria are useful for our golden innovations as well.

Based on similar successful principles of empowerment through positive affirmation, David L. Cooperrider, associate professor of

Organizational Behavior at Case Western Reserve University, has developed a powerful social innovation for organizational development and transformation called appreciative inquiry — an inquiry into what we appreciate, affirm, and desire to cocreate in our future. He wrote in a paper entitled "Appreciative Inquiry: A Constructive Approach to Organizational Development and Change,"

> We have reached the "end of problem solving" as a mode of inquiry capable of inspiring, mobilizing, and sustaining human system change. The future of organizational development belongs to methods that affirm, compel, and accelerate anticipatory learning involving larger and larger levels of collectivity. The new methods will be distinguished by the art and the science of asking powerful, positive questions. The new methods will view realities as socially constructed and will therefore become more radically relational, widening the circle of dialogue to groups of 100s, 1000s, and perhaps more — with cyberspace relationships into the millions. . . . The arduous tasks of intervention will give way to the speed of imagination and innovation; and instead of negation, criticism, and spiraling diagnosis, there will be discovery, dream, design, and destiny.[5]

Can you imagine appreciative inquiries concerning what works on the Internet involving millions of people? Is this not potentially a fundamental innovation leading toward the next stage of self-organization and democracy?

These examples and thousands more are based on faith in the goodness of human nature when we are placed in win-win social systems that bring out the best in us. Although a low-synergy, win-lose situation tends to bring out our worst traits, a win-win, high-synergy social system brings out our creativity and responsibility. As Maslow and the human potential movement affirmed the innate goodness of people, so these social innovations affirm and design systems that call forth our better nature in groups and in community. Imagine a continuous flow of such golden innovations entering the wheel in each sector of the living system. It is the new body politic coming alive.

GLOBAL COLLEGIUM

The Global Collegium is an ever-expanding network of individuals knowledgable in their fields about innovations now working to heal and evolve our world. They help identify breakthroughs and systemic changes. They are willing to evaluate, select, foster, nurture and study innovations that work.

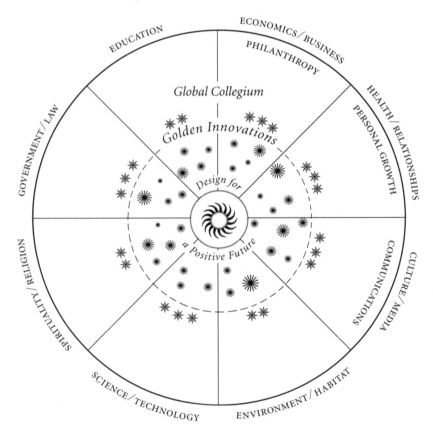

✳ = Global Collegium
✳ = Golden Innovations

The Global Collegium

How will we locate golden innovations? How can we be assured that the innovations wheel website will gather into its global brain and heart projects now changing the world for the good? One way is through the formation of an ever-expanding, self-selected global collegium composed of faithful mappers and trackers of the emerging integral culture, individuals with sapiential authority — the authority of actually knowing what is working. The collegium will continually scan for and map golden innovations to discover how we are cocreating our new civilization.

Even fifty outstanding people who know their respective fields and are each connected to twenty others could keep the wheel informed and in touch with the pureness of golden innovations. Remember the nature of dissipative structures: when the interactions become nonlinear and exponential, the system can repattern itself rapidly.

But we are by no means starting from the beginning. I rejoice to say that many such people are already at work and have highly developed websites, extended networks, and wide arenas of influence at the growing edge of change. Because of the rapid rise of the Internet, the number of websites working on aspects of this new function is mounting daily. Since my campaign for a positive future, this meme has been taking root. Here are some examples.

Jerome Clayton Glenn (who was a director of The Committee for the Future) is now codirector with futurist Theodore Gordon of the American Council for The United Nations University's Millennium Project, a worldwide effort to collect and synthesize judgments about emerging global issues and opportunities that may affect the human condition.[6] This year's study extends previous work and builds on its findings, emphasizing positive developments.

Eleanor LeCain, who served as a Massachusetts assistant under secretary of state for long range planning, is director of the Campaign for What Works. She has been researching golden innovations in a variety of fields from education to business to crime for her book and has identified key golden innovations that could transform every field:

> If we adapted and adopted these innovations more widely, we could save billions of dollars and improve the quality of life for millions of people. The Campaign for What Works should build support for having the best of what works in every community. Through the Campaign, I will bring together the people who created the golden innovations to share expertise and insights across fields. We will encourage citizens to scan for what works in their community, and share that information across the country. We will support candidates for public office who are serious about building on what works. By building on proven programs that already exist, we can transform the country in this generation.[7]

Rena Shulsky, founder of Green Seal, founder and cochair of the 1990 Swords Into Plowshares Conference, and a founding member of Social Venture Network has established The Center for What Works.[8] Its executive director is Jason Saul. The center is a major step toward our vision of the Campaign for What Works. Its mission is to research, catalog, and disseminate information about successful social programs around the country and the world. The center studies what's right with social programs and how to replicate them. It is as a nonpartisan international clearinghouse for cost-effective solutions with a proven track record of success. It represents the first real effort to benchmark and evaluate the best practices in social policy. It serves four constituencies: public, government, and policy makers; corporations; nonprofits; and foundations.

Marianne Williamson, author of *A Return to Love* and *The Healing of America*, has founded The American Renaissance Alliance to offer citizens actions for holistic politics — how to bring our highest values into action in the political field. She wrote in *The Healing of America*,

> Within the next ten years America will experience a renaissance or a catastrophe. Something is going to happen to take us back to who we are.... It is time once more for the average American citizen to turn to the dominant power structure of our time and say, as did our Founders over two hundred years ago: We have a better idea.[9]

Marianne is working with Eleanor LeCain and many others to design a program for holistic political action.

Corinne McLaughlin and Gordon Davidson of the Center for Visionary Leadership in Washington, D.C., are already identifying projects that work, both in their book *Spiritual Politics* and in their newsletter, which not only selects individual breakthroughs, but seeks to abstract from them the principles and practices of workability.[10]

Barbara Pyle of CNN has been researching projects that work to discuss on television, an effort inspired in part by Planet Live, an initiative Hazel Henderson and I launched with Ted Turner, an early version of the NewNews described in Chapter 13.

Many major organizations, such as the United Nations, are developing best practices websites, collecting data on what is working in every major field of endeavor. (Refer to Resources in Part 5: A Call to Action for websites on organizations mentioned, as well as many others.)

This is not a dream of the future. Countless good works and breakthroughs are now happening. The global collegium will eventually include an ever-expanding group of creative innovators and mappers throughout the entire system.

A Rising Tide

Just imagine even fifty major innovators coming together to identify golden innovations and to connect the wheel with their extensive networks. Very rapidly we would see the outlines of the new world. We are now at the threshold of the dynamic moment in history when we can facilitate the gentle repatterning of our society.

To help manifest this new social function, Mark Donohue, Eleanor LeCain, and I have envisioned holding a forum called The Innovation and Leadership Initiative, which would bring together leading social innovators in crucial fields of human endeavor. They would be joined by leading mappers of progress, so that we would embody a cocreative collaboration at the frontier of the emerging world. Mappers would represent organizations such as the Nobel Prize Committee, the MacArthur Foundation, and the Kyoto Prize, which separately recognize breakthroughs in the fields of peace, science, social innovation, and more; Civicus, the largest mapper of civil society's successes; the Social Venture Network, the leading global organization tracking and representing socially responsible businesses; the Arias Foundation and Carter Center, which monitor conflict resolution and disarmament initiatives; and about fifty other leading organizations, each expert in tracking social innovations. This event would bring together the most advanced resources and understanding of where human innovation, aspiration, and perspiration are positively transforming the world. We would do much more than network as we synergistically work on bringing forth a global database of the most exciting projects in human endeavor.

Our forum would also invite the leading international scholars of diffusion (marketing) research so that innovators and mappers can learn the most effective techniques to spread positive initiatives globally. Marketing research will no longer be used primarily by multinational marketing conglomerates.

Social progress can no longer be engineered solely through large bureaucracies or centralized management. Another sector of human endeavor, civil society, would now take its place as a full partner in the new leadership as shown by our map of leaders in progress. Our vision is that the Innovation and Leadership Initiative would give a clear voice to the creativity of humanity and would fully establish this new social function both on the Internet and in the world.

As Archimedes said, "If we have the right fulcrum point, we can move the world." What finer place to position ourselves than at the creative frontier of humanity? The Innovation and Leadership Initiative would be a project that fully honors our technological brilliance and human potential.

We also envision the forum as the basis for a global media event. Our message for the generally disinterested media would be, "In one room, we will gather more knowledge of humanity's progress and success than has ever been assembled in the history of all time." This event would offer a true opportunity for media to finally be used for its highest evolutionary purpose.

Community of Cocreators

Golden innovations and the ever-growing global collegium form one vital aspect of the new social process. Its dynamism and power come from the community of cocreators — social innovators and builders of the new world — you and me. People everywhere enter their projects at whatever stage they are, provided that they are in alignment with the core values of conscious evolution. For example, if a project is based on violence or on racial or ethnic prejudice, if it is destructive to the environment, it does not belong in the wheel.

GLOBAL COLLEGIUM

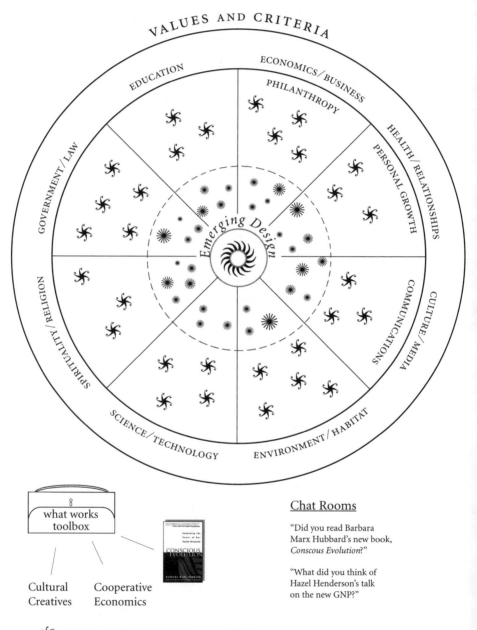

Chat Rooms

"Did you read Barbara Marx Hubbard's new book, *Conscous Evolution*?"

"What did you think of Hazel Henderson's talk on the new GNP?"

Eventually, project initiators can learn about golden innovations in their fields to obtain the best guidelines available for stimulating individual creativity. These links to already existing website databases of the best practices in every sector, such as health, education, and environment, can serve as a great reservoir of existing knowledge of what works. (Some databases are listed in Part 5: A Call to Action.)

We needn't reinvent the wheel when we begin a new project. We can build on successes throughout the system. For example, if there is a breakthrough in our scientific laboratories, it is quickly communicated to other scientists around the world. Yet, in the realm of social innovations, there is no comparable process. In fact, many people in the same town where a breakthrough innovation exists often don't know of the progress in their midst.

The wheel will be an important learning process and will be an inherent part of the education for conscious evolution. Through it we can study the patterns of success, the people, criteria, experiences, and circumstances now working toward the world we choose. The essence of the Campaign for What Works is to build greater coherence and alignment within the peaks of our accumulated knowledge through the conscious connecting of the converging elements. This process will follow in the model Prigogine brought forth, whereby living systems "escape" into higher order and greater freedom through the increased interaction among innovations.

As Maslow began the human potential movement by studying healthy people, we can now further empower the social potential movement by learning from, connecting, and amplifying healthy social innovations, continually building upon what works.

Community of CoCreators

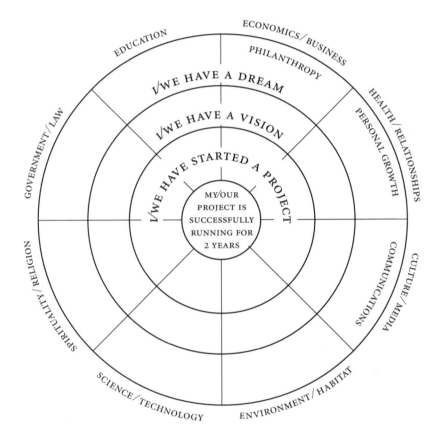

The center of the wheel is the space for the nonlinear, exponential interaction among innovating elements, where the repatterning described by Prigogine happens naturally and spontaneously. It is a convergence zone for what works, both on the Internet and in convenings to facilitate the interactions and communication of the positive. In the center of the wheel we place the golden innovations and seek to discover how these innovations function in a mutually synergistic way. It is an arena for synthesis and fusion of genius.

From time to time the collegium should be brought together to listen carefully to one another, to seek the metapattern that connects, and to help discover the design of evolution for further communication and study. Beyond policy proposals, political platforms, and ideological-based solutions, the people would construct a blueprint based on pragmatic success in each functional area of the emerging society. Symbolically, it would be a planetary DNA or memetic code of the next development of the social body. This ever-evolving design would be communicated as widely as possible. As people from all over the world begin their projects, look for common goals, match needs and resources, connect with others, and dialog with the collegium, the community of cocreators develops.

Spirit at the Center

The center of the wheel is symbolically a temple for the templates, the models that work, the individual memes forming the mother meme of our conscious evolution. It is a place where we dare to have complete faith in our positive future.

At the center of the wheel, Spirit dwells — the invisible force that connects us in the web of life itself. The center is symbolically a sacred space, an inner peace room where we come to the still point within ourselves, embodying the unmanifest field of all possibilities.

Here we allow Spirit to connect us. In the center of the symbolic wheel, we come together as pioneering souls; we are silent, we listen, we attune; we share at the soul level what we know is right and good. We see how we can better coordinate our acts with others and with the larger process of creation.

The center of the wheel is seen symbolically as a place in consciousness where the accumulated wisdom of the whole process of creation is focused and becomes conscious in us. The center is informed by the spiral of evolution of the past and gives rise to the yet unrealized turns of the spiral in the future. We become aware that each of us is participating in an ever-evolving creation as conscious cocreators. We can see the wheel as a process of convergence representing our turn on the spiral and each of us liberated to express our creativity within the whole, leading toward endless transformation, beyond us, in this universe without end.

Conscious Evolution:

A Spirit-Motivated Plan of Action
for the 21st Century

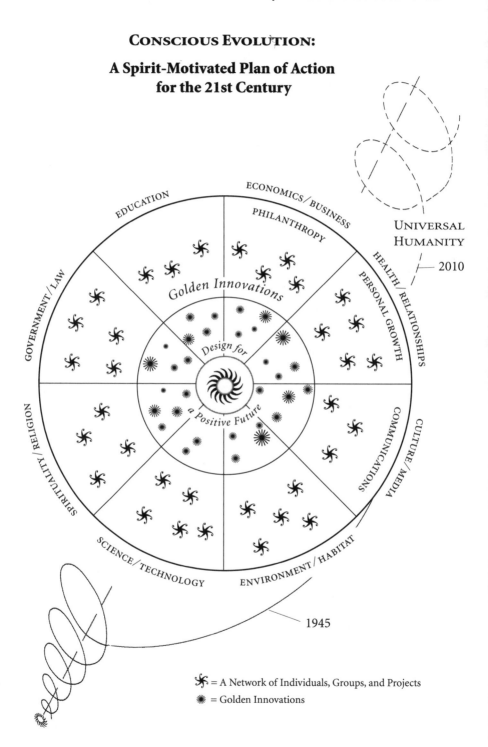

Golden Innovations

Design for

a Positive Future

EDUCATION
ECONOMICS/BUSINESS
PHILANTHROPY
GOVERNMENT/LAW
HEALTH/RELATIONSHIPS
PERSONAL GROWTH
SPIRITUALITY/RELIGION
COMMUNICATIONS
CULTURE/MEDIA
SCIENCE/TECHNOLOGY
ENVIRONMENT/HABITAT

UNIVERSAL
HUMANITY
2010

1945

✹ = A Network of Individuals, Groups, and Projects
✳ = Golden Innovations

CHAPTER TWELVE

A Pattern of Transformation Revealed

P rigogine described how nature has evolved from simple to more complex through (among other factors) the increased and novel interactions within a highly nonequilibrium system, resulting in a quantum jump, a repatterning to a higher order. The new social function we are describing will facilitate our social system to make such a jump through providing the opportunity for greater and more coherent interactions among innovating elements.

As we have seen, our global society can be viewed as a large dissipative structure that is increasingly undergoing perturbations. On the one hand, there is an acceleration of breakdowns. On the other hand, breakthroughs are arising everywhere. We can see that every sector of the innovations wheel is actually a strand of the evolutionary agenda that is rising toward convergence. (The center of the innovations wheel, where the planetary DNA or design for a positive future comes together, is the convergence zone of the Prigogine model. See page 106.)

The acceleration of breakdowns in our system, such as population growth, hunger, poverty, violence, environmental decay, toxic wastes, the greenhouse effect, and pollution of the seas and the soil, are mutually interactive and lead to increased entropy or disorder in the system. Some scientists have predicted that because of the rapidly increasing interactions among breakdowns, we may cause irreversible damage to our life system in a very short period of time.

What is almost never noticed, however, is that there is a concurrent convergence of positive social innovations. It is a matter of timing as to which happens first: the exponential convergence of the breakdowns or the breakthroughs (which will become critical and cause the quantum change). Will we go downward toward devolution or upward toward evolutionary transformation and metamorphosis?

If the positive innovations connect exponentially before the massive breakdowns reinforce one another, the system can repattern itself to a higher order of consciousness and freedom without the predicted economic, environmental, or social collapse. We can evolve toward the positive as quickly as we might devolve toward the negative because of the phenomenon of nonlinear exponential interactions. If the system could go either way, a slight intervention to assist the convergence of the positive can tip the scales of evolution in favor of the enhancement of life on Earth. Therefore, the essence of our plan of action is to consciously accelerate the convergence of positive awareness and action.

Catastrophe and creation are twins. If we make a scroll of the Priogine diagram, we can see that the catastrophic breakdown of the old system (the social caterpillar) is vital to the creative metamorphosis of the new system (the societal butterfly).

As the awareness of what is not working grows, more and more people want to jump toward what is working. The higher order is thus composed of the restructuring of the disintegrating old order. More imaginal cells appear in the social body, attracted by the promise of greater fulfillment and by the joys of cocreation. In this regard, part of the work of the social potential movement is to create new vocational paths for these pioneering souls.

Our plan of action is designed to facilitate what is natural, but is being restricted by divisiveness in our system such as the competition and violence among religions and nations, the separation of the disciplines within education, and the mass media's emphasis on breakdowns, and dysfunctional, disempowering, organizational structures.

Where We Are Now

We are in a period of dramatic increased instability, confusion, loss of vision. Tension is increasing everywhere as the old order struggles to prevail and the new order tries to emerge. We are in what may be called the "tension zone," as indicated in the diagram on page 106. Innovators run into complexities and difficulties, both in the external world through resistant social systems and through immaturities, addictions, and egotism within themselves.

As the climb gets steeper, any flaws in our character will show up. To enter the convergence zone as those who are responsible for social innovations, we must become mature imaginal cells. It is a time for continued self-improvement. In fact, the social potential movement gives new meaning to the 30-year effort of millions within the human potential movement. To take the next step we must become more conscious of our own state of being — of our thoughts and intentions. For as we approach the convergence zone, everything within us is magnified, our weaknesses as well as our strengths.

The pressure on all social change agents is intense. We continue to struggle to evolve — personally, financially, organizationally — usually with little support from our current culture. Many of us may fall by the wayside, at least for the moment. But those who persevere through the tension zone have a great reward in store for all of us. For once inside the convergence zone new patterns prevail and reinforce one another, and we get a taste of the cocreative society — heaven on Earth.

Practicing the personal path of the cocreator is vital, for we must stabilize our own higher internal state of being to remain in the convergence zone. Most particularly, we seek to overcome our ego-driven behavior — our desire to dominate and win over others — and learn to cooperate and cocreate. Few of us have learned to remain in our higher state of being. We are competitive and have a desire to win. We lose resonance, we fear rejection, judgment seeps in, and we fall into separation — then struggle to rise again and again, seeking to stabilize. Very few of us have stabilized at our own high norm (certainly including me). We flicker in and out of higher consciousness. But remember, we are still a young species. I believe that we have not yet discovered what it means to be fully human. This is the work of the maturing social potential movement: to provide win-win social systems within which the higher qualities of love, creativity, and the responsibility of humanity can be reinforced and secured.

The Joys of Cocreation

When we enter the convergence zone, our new state of being as cocreators is enhanced and stabilized. We experience the joys of cocreation. We have all felt this magnificent state in flashes of peak experiences, when we are in the flow, in the zone, in the swing of things. It occurs whenever two or more pioneering souls (imaginal cells) are drawn together to cocreate, to fuse genius, to work on an activity that actualizes each person's unique potential. In those moments we experience resonance, a re-sounding, or echoing, of each other's higher qualities. This wonderful feeling affirms and reinforces each person's creativity.

Dissonance and resistance dissolve when we fuse our genius. Convergence eats entropy. Two or more gathered in resonance form the basic building block of the integral culture. In this field of resonance, our self-expression is amplified and flows naturally. Nature has built in an incentive for cocreation just as she has for procreation. It is pleasure. In the convergence zone, we do not solve our problems in the same state of consciousness in which we created them. For in the process of coming together to solve problems, we ourselves are changed, our genius codes join, and something greater than ourselves emerges from our union with other kindred souls.

The Four Ss

When we are in the convergence zone, the Four Ss prevail: synergy, synchronicity, syntony, and suprasex. The joy intensifies, we feel social ease, laughter, fun, and effortlessness. Let's see what the Four Ss teach us.

1. Synergy. Synergy is the experience that we are part of a larger group or social body. It is the glorious sense of becoming ourselves more fully through deeper participation with others. In a synergistic team, all we need to do is our part and allow and encourage others to do their parts. Our part becomes amplified and fulfilled through

joining with others, who are experiencing the same fulfillment of their unique parts through joining with us. The words "love your neighbor as yourself" become a reality. The other is part of oneself. In synergy we recognize that we are members of a larger whole; the dichotomy between self and other is overcome. The illusion of separation dissolves as the uniqueness of each person increases through participation in the greater whole.

By the alignment among all members of the body, the binding force of nature, grace, Spirit — whatever name we call it — joins us as part of a larger whole in which we, as separate parts, mysteriously feel more uniquely ourselves than ever before. The word "cooperation" changes its meaning from helping one another to being members of one body coordinated by the larger process of creation.

In the convergence zone we enter a flow state, defined by Mihaly Csikszentmihalyi in *The Evolving Self* as one in which we are using all our capacities to realize a goal of intrinsic value,

> Flow usually occurs when there are clear goals a person tries to reach and when there is unambiguous feedback as to how well he or she is doing.... When we enjoy it, it is because we think of it as something that allows us to express our potential, to learn about our limits, to stretch our being. It is for this reason that flow is such an important force in evolution. Without it, our genetic programs would instruct us to continue pursuing what has been "good for us" in the past; but flow makes us receptive to the entire world as a source of new challenges, as an arena for creativity.... It is an escape forward into higher complexity, where one hones one's potential by confronting new challenges. Because the fine balance between challenge and skill makes it necessary to concentrate on the task at hand, people in flow report a loss of self-consciousness.[1]

In other words, the experience of separateness and awareness of self as a separate being dissolves in the flow state. A more unitive form of consciousness is momentarily achieved. The SYNCON process brings people together to share their passions, to create, and match their needs and resources (see page 226).

2. Synchronicity. Carl Jung defined it in *Synchronicity: An Acasual Connecting Principle* as "a meaningful coincidence of two or more events, where something other than the probability of chance is involved."[2] In the convergence zone, synchronicities increase. The timing is not in our hands; events seem to occur as needed. Complexities that could not be planned for appear to self-organize. There is a sense of effortlessness although everyone is working very hard.

People we are looking for are often looking for us. We ask a question and the answer comes quickly, often in strange and unexpected ways. When we are in the flow there is the feeling of being organized by the deeper pattern rather than by having to make things happen by will and linear planning alone. We still plan and execute, but with a feeling of grace and support rather than by will alone. We feel we are coordinated by the whole of which we are a part. This feeling may be accurate, for in the flow state we are more sensitive to the deeper tendency in evolution toward higher consciousness and greater freedom.

3. Syntony. This term, coined by Eric Jantsch in his book *Design for Evolution*, described one of the ways of accessing conscious evolution, as mentioned earlier.[3] The relationship between the cosmic design and the individual intensifies through some form of syntony or resonance. Syntony feels like guidance, intuition, or direct knowing. We do not have to figure out what to do. We know. We perform

with spontaneous right action. The inner world of subjective experience and the outer world of objective reality blend and become one. We and the world "outside us" are interconnected in one larger field of intelligence. The great flashes of awareness that mystics have experienced throughout history are reinforced and normalized. Each of us becomes more attuned to the deeper patterns; intuition and intellect blend. The mystical state becomes grounded and manifested in spirit-motivated social action.

4. Suprasex. The next stage of sexuality, suprasex, occurs when our genius is aroused and we desire to join our genius to cocreate. Suprasexual passion increases in the convergence zone. We are vocationally aroused at the level of our genius. Instead of joining our genes to have a child, we join our genius to give birth to our full potential selves and to the work that expresses our combined love. Energy floods into our systems. Procreation extends itself into cocreation. We do not tire as easily or get sick as often. We feel exhilarated, light hearted, and exuberant. Even our sexuality is enhanced, not to have a child, but to "have ourselves," to regenerate ourselves through love. Yet the emphasis is not on sexuality; it is on creativity. Brilliant ideas are triggered by the presence of others who reinforce our own potential.

Possessiveness and self-centeredness dissolve for the moment, not out of self-sacrifice, but out of self-fulfillment through cocreation. The ego is absorbed through expressing its uniqueness. The poison of selfishness is dissolved as we give our best in such a way that both we as individuals and as others are blessed by our creativity.

In certain moments of convergence, we experience the ecstasy of cocreation. It feels as though we are one with the creator within ourselves and our partners, which transcends the self-centered individual. In the act of expressing our genius and of being received in love by other members of the whole, we feel as though we've come home at last, no longer alien and cast out in unfamiliar surroundings, as we give of ourselves lovingly and we are received in love. This is a form of "social love" possible in a cocreative world. It combines "eros," erotic love, and "agape," altruistic love, arousing our passion at all levels of being.

At our current stage of evolution, we are deeply drawn to stabilize the experience, not as an ecstatic high but as a new normalcy. We proceed by making normal what was first a peak experience. The pleasure principle is intrinsic to social evolution. We do not evolve the world by guilt and duty any more than we populated the world through such feelings!

Our social structures often separate us, keeping us from our natural desire to cocreate. We simply haven't known that social convergence is the key to our heart's desire. We are separated into disciplines, fields, mind sets, ideologies, colors, races, economic classes, and religions. Our communities and families are breaking apart, and we are often lonely, isolated, and purposeless. For lack of something exciting to attract us forward, many of us are looking backward to our ethnic roots for exclusive identity. We have not created systems to help us find our teammates, partners, and social cocreators at local or regional levels. Few places are designed specifically for joining our genius and giving birth to our projects and gifts to the world.

Yet, we can see that the process of evolution tends to favor our higher consciousness, our greater freedom, and our efforts toward a win-win synergistic society. Every such intention and action is reinforced by the tendency in evolution that has been moving forward for billions of years. Although there is freedom in the system, and increasingly so, it is also true that the universe is designed to select and enhance higher states of being and doing, as it has demonstrated in the progression from molecule to cell to animal to human to the great avatars, and now to us attempting to become a universal, cocreative species. From the perspective of conscious evolution, we are not operating in a vacuum or in a neutral universe, but in a universal living system animated everywhere with intelligence, growing toward higher consciousness and freedom. It is this intelligence that we are becoming aware of in us, as us, as we practice our own conscious evolution.

Our passion to create and self-express is always driving us toward convergence. The drive for self-preservation and self-reproduction are merging into Maslow's third drive — self-actualization — giving us the fuel to forge the evolutionary frontier. We invented the jury, the vote, the town meeting, the Bill of Rights for the first phase of freedom, and now we are inventing a new social architecture for cocreation.

CHAPTER THIRTEEN

The NewNews

L et's imagine that the social potential movement is emerging and gathering strength. Teams have formed to act as catalysts to help bring the process into focus. Now what is needed to make the system work is the maturation of our mass media, our planetary nervous system. We must see images of social wellness if we are to have the faith and courage to heal our society and grow. Consider for a moment that a newborn child is surrounded by those who think it is ugly and who notice only its weaknesses, messes, and failures. Think how it would be affected. We are a newly emerged planetary society, and we need to make sure we are receiving positive feedback. We need at least one extraordinary media outreach that can set the new template and affect all other media.

The NewNews: A Channel for Cocreation

The single most important thing we could do with the media is offer a new conception of what we mean by news. Many people believe what they see on the news is the truth. For this evolutionary plan to succeed we need to cocreate the NewNews. We have already envisioned the movement for what works spreading throughout the world via rapidly increasing networking among innovators. Now let's build on that and imagine a television show called "The NewNews: What's Working in the World." It is real "tell-a-vision" also available on radio, or it might even start on radio. It is a megaphone for creative breakthroughs and successes, which invites millions of people to participate in constructive action.

The NewNews is the real life drama of the human family's struggle to evolve. It takes place in a live "situation room" fed by the cocreation website and all other sources of good news and good works. The feeling is one of genuine excitement, danger, and opportunity, because the real question is, evolution or extinction? Will we make it through this critical period or won't we? Our initiators are seen as genuine heroes and heroines, the true newsmakers of our time. The NewNews invites all of us to start on the hero's path.

Guests come on the show to report what's working. Golden innovations are dramatized, especially from the personal point of view. How did you do it? How did your family respond? How did you support yourself? Where did you suffer? What did you enjoy? We see our visions and our social goals in a section of the NewNews entitled "Visions of a Positive Future." People are invited to send in their visions of the new world so that tell-a-vision can collect them and continually report to viewers the future they are choosing.

We use techniques similar to those David Ellis offered in his book, *Creating Your Future*, urging people to project into the long-range future to overcome self-imposed limitations.[1] We begin collectively to do what James Redfield described in *The Tenth Insight* and in *The Celestine Vision*.[2] We "hold the vision," built of all our choices, potentials, and pragmatic successes. By placing our ever-expanding and enriching vision on the news (and on the Internet), we begin to see it as real and are thereby further activated to realize it now in our lives. It is not something in the future we are waiting for, but rather a stimulus to awaken our creativity in the present. What we envision we begin to create.

The hosts of the NewNews pay particular attention when adversaries begin to agree on something, for finding common ground is one of the foundational elements of the emerging culture. For example, I remember a specially designed SYNCON, or synergistic convergence conference, produced by the Committee for the Future, which we put on for gang leaders in the inner city of Los Angeles. (The Committee for the Future produced twenty-five such synergistic conferences from 1972 to 1976.) We gathered together the leading gangs of Los Angeles: Hispanic, Asian, African-American, and white. The process was designed to have people state their passions to create; their goals, needs, and resources, and to seek common goals in a wheel-shaped environment divided into sectors, as in the innovations wheel. The police, welfare recipients, former convicts, shopkeepers, crime victims, corporate executives, and science fiction writers like Ray Bradbury and Gene Roddenberry were also present.

At one point we felt a sense of something new and fragile coming together. Each task force stated its goals, what it needed to accomplish the goals, and the resources it could offer to others. The police and corporate executives were paying close attention to the kids' words. All participants met as equal members of the community trying to work out something together. One black gang leader was standing in the center of the circle in his worn leather jacket. He had been quiet and looked depressed throughout the 3-day event.

Suddenly he took a deep breath and spoke in a voice so soft that all of us had to lean toward him to hear. "I think it's going to be all right, we're going to be heard..." he said.

In that instant an ABC-TV camera crew arrived. They started to pull gang members aside to find out what was going on. The young black leader who had just spoken faced the TV cameras and said loudly for all to hear: "Go away! We won't let you do this to us again. We won't let you make us look bad. Go away!"

The mass media cameras retreated, our little handheld camera zoomed in on the young man, and we heard his story, for the first time, of how the media had distorted gangs by always communicating their worst behavior. We began to discuss important issues with the members of those gangs. It was a very powerful and moving experience as they started to communicate. My partner at the time, the late John Whiteside, created "The New World Evening News," in which he played back the peaks of new agreements and acts of cooperation that occurred on that day. People were fascinated to see themselves as newsmakers and wanted to watch the program over and over. "The New World Evening News" format and approach can be incorporated into the NewNews.

A major 24-hour-a-day "human potential television" channel is close to manifestation. It would have programming focusing on such themes as living as a whole person, lifelong learning, personal growth, vocational development, spirituality, what's working to create a better world, and personal stories of our new leaders in progress.

The Wisdom Channel is already up and running. Launched on July 1, 1997, it is a new satellite network dedicated to personal growth and the human potential movement. It includes television, radio, and Internet channels and is delivered currently via C-Band satellite, available to approximately 4.3 million households in the United States, Canada, Mexico, and parts of South America and the Caribbean.

Michael Toms' New Dimensions Radio has been collecting interviews with people at the leading edge for more than 25 years, distributed to more than 250 public radio stations in the United States, and available internationally via short wave on Radio for Peace International. New Dimensions will be carried via the Wisdom Channel.

WETV: The Global Access Television Network delivers an underlying message about the environment and sustainable development, cultural diversity, and the empowerment of women and youth. WETV acquires, produces, and distributes this innovative programming via satellite to broadcast affiliates throughout the world.

This and other such efforts are favorably disposed to the NewNews idea. It is only a matter of time, energy, and focus to make it happen at a comprehensive and popular scale required to reach the general public.

Another powerful form of media is the arts. Artists are essential to the NewNews — to inspire, reveal, and illuminate what is happening. Poets, dancers, painters, and musicians weave a web of meaning and revelation throughout the NewNews show. Earl Hubbard's statement made so long ago in the little cafe on the Left Bank — "we need artists to tell us our new story" — comes true on the NewNews. We find creative talent that has been blocked from expression by the limited access and negative self-image prevalent in popular culture. Our birth as universal humanity calls forth an outpouring of creativity as our new self-images, visions, and dreams are portrayed by artistic genius.

Through the technology of computer animation, we have the breathtaking ability to dramatize and make our visions real. Seeing is believing. Advanced art forms are a vital part of cocreating the future.

Through the NewNews program, viewers will be invited to turn on their computers and place their projects, their dreams, and their visions on the website. The website should develop a service for matching needs with resources through a vocational dating service spotlighted by the NewNews. This function will help people find their teammates, their partners, and their projects, stirring the creative energy latent in millions. Vocational arousal sweeps the nation, the world, and the NewNews goes global. We could find ourselves in the midst of a social uprising of wellness.

What do you suppose happens to the other news shows when the NewNews becomes popular? They start to compete. Reporters are told to find out what's working. Muckrakers become pearlrakers. Yellow journalism becomes silver and gold! People start noticing what's working in their own lives. The NewNews is flooded with stories of what works from all around the world. (Already, Peter Jennings, the commentator for ABC national news, has introduced into the evening news a segment called "Solutions," which highlights innovations and breakthroughs.)

Let's imagine that the NewNews becomes a popular TV show, broadcast worldwide. Situation comedies, dramas, and documentaries soon follow the news, revealing the numberless stories of the frontiers of human progress. The social potential movement is launched.

Everywhere people are calling in, asking how they can learn to be cocreators, how they can become social innovators, how they can help. The stage is set for a new education in conscious evolution.

CHAPTER FOURTEEN

Education for Conscious Evolution

Education for conscious evolution is the context in which all disciplines and fields work together to understand and guide the evolution of humanity. It is the metadiscipline we need to provide the knowledge, motivation, and opportunities upon which leadership in the 21st century will form.

Ralph Abraham, the renowned chaos theorist and mathematician, highlighted the necessity for an education in conscious evolution. In *Chaos, Gaia, Eros* he wrote,

> Here is the crux of the world problem. Its evolution — *cultural evolution*, or *sociogenesis* — is subject to the laws of general evolution theory. As we learn laws from comparative studies in the histories of geogenesis, biogenesis, and noogenesis, we may develop the capability to guide our own sociogenesis, and to participate in the creation of our future. This points to a new science of the future, a *true* social science, with mathematical models and observational laws, with understanding and wisdom, and with a basis in history and social philosophy.[1]

As we have seen, the first part of the plan is to understand our new story of creation and our new meme of conscious evolution. Then comes the formation of a new social architecture to facilitate the communication and convergence of positive actions. We have envisioned a Campaign for What Works supported by a website that scans for, maps, connects, and communicates breakthroughs in every field. We envisioned a global collegium of outstanding innovators at every level — local, regional, and global — who are seeking out innovations currently changing the system. They are piecing together an ever-evolving design for a positive future based on synergy among innovations. A vast community on the Internet is participating in the discovery, empowerment, and replication of what is working in every field. And finally, we envisioned a continuing broadcasting of breakthroughs and successes over the NewNews and all other available media to educate our society on the positive changes occurring — inviting public participation in what works. This process is the basis for a new education for conscious evolution.

Now, let's imagine that millions of people are inspired by what they see and hear is happening throughout the world and they want to participate. Where do people learn to be social innovators? Who can assist them in discovering their evolutionary vocations and in entering the lifelong learning process of cocreation?

In 5th-century Greece there was the agora — the marketplace of ideas, a popular assembly site where Socrates and Plato held their famous dialogues to challenge students' beliefs. The foundation of philosophy, ethics, and metaphysics were laid out. Later, in medieval times, universities emerged. They were great preservers and communicators of knowledge.

Our modern universities are still structured in the medieval model — divided into disciplines and fields — with scant integrative orientation to guide us to develop the visions, purposes, and goals of humanity as a whole entering the first age of conscious evolution. Many teachers and isolated curricula are occurring throughout society that offer aspects of conscious evolution (described in Part 5: A Call to Action). Workshops, seminars, and trainings proliferate. Yet, these brilliant educational initiatives are scattered, disconnected, and often unknown to students who want to learn. For all the experimentation in education, we are still limited to an antiquated educational framework that offers little relationship among disciplines and gives little opportunity for students to ask the ultimate questions about our destiny and how they can participate in creating a positive future.

As a young and unsuspecting imaginal cell, I had no idea of my vocation; I looked at all the separate courses — English, history, science, art — each in an unrelated box, but couldn't relate the courses to my quest for life purpose. I did not know what I wanted to do or be. I had a slight glimmer, which most of us have, yet found no way to nourish my faint vision. I wrote in my journal for the first time in May 1948, when I was eighteen years old and a sophomore in college,

> I've waited far too long to begin my journal. Feelings, intuitions, ideas have been lost irrevocably. I have a desperate need to create. All my life I have absorbed. By using myself as a catalytic agent, I hope to give pattern and form to the mass of sensations that have impressed themselves upon me. The power of intelligence is to connect, to relate, and to integrate impressions. If there is a God, it is One who unites past with present and future, finite with infinite, truths with apparently conflicting truths, until all are more than a conglomeration, all is one and that one is far greater than the sum of its parts. That one is God's creation.[2]

Given the broad and undefined nature of my quest, how could I choose what to major in, much less what to minor in? There was nothing seemingly available to facilitate the discovery of my life purpose. My roommate, whom I had just met, suggested that we go to Washington to get a job after college. I agreed and therefore chose political science for my major. It was that haphazard.

You may say that my search for meaning was somewhat obsessive, but I believe we all have the same need to find what we are born to do and where we are needed to do it.

Eventually, as I found my vocation, my father would say, "Barbara, you're the best in the field — but there's no field!" Recently, Prof. A. Harris Stone put it this way when he asked me to write a rationale for the new field of conscious evolution: "There is a body of knowledge, but there is no field." We need to establish this new field of thought so it can be introduced into the academic community as well as into the social and political communities, thus enabling proper research that will in turn make the body of knowledge accessible to the brightest minds of our time. But it is often difficult, if not impossible, to introduce something new into an old form. It is now time to bring together those who have the vision, and the passion, to develop the curriculum for conscious evolution. Even now many people are at work teaching, often hidden within more traditional systems. When the larger context is established to create a new educational system, these innovators will be ready to add to the curriculum for conscious evolution.

A Metadiscipline for the 21st Century

Because all disciplines are needed to understand and guide ethical evolution, the commitment to conscious evolution will help us break out of the boxes of separate disciplines structured so deeply into our academic institutions. The metadiscipline of conscious evolution offers us a coherent matrix in which all our disciplines fit. The framework is the evolutionary spiral seen as the process of creation now continuing through us, in what Duane Elgin called a continuous creation — seeing our futures as a continuum of this process unfolding into an ever-expanding horizon of no known limits. All functions are interrelated, as in any living body. Through the metadiscipline of conscious evolution, we greatly enhance our understanding of how to cocreate new systems appropriate for this stage of evolution.

Cosmology, geology, anthropology, history, science and technology, psychology, art, and current affairs are not separate subjects, but interrelated processes that have brought us to this point of evolution. In the context of conscious evolution students in the various disciplines would have to converge in an effort to understand how to evolve consciously. Gregory Bateson wrote in the introduction to *Mind and Nature, A Necessary Unity*, "What is the pattern which connects all the living creatures? . . . The pattern which connects is a meta-pattern. It is a pattern of patterns."[3] It is this metapattern that the metadiscipline of education for conscious evolution seeks to understand and apply to guide our actions in the coming millennium.

What we need now is a conscious evolution "project" to facilitate and gently guide the quantum jump. The coming 50 years should be dedicated to bringing together the intellectual, social, and spiritual resources of our brilliant species to lay the foundations for the next stage of human evolution as now undertaken by the Foundation for the Future (see page 253).

In this coherent context the scattered parts of knowledge could come together and form the field of conscious evolution.

A New School for Conscious Evolution

To house the new metadiscipline, new schools for conscious evolution are needed, not only a school of thought, but also school sites, whether in accredited universities or not, where people gather to teach and learn how to participate in conscious evolution — spiritually, socially, and scientifically. Schools for conscious evolution would provide students (meaning all of us) with knowledge, connections, mentors, and skills needed to fulfill our vocations of destiny in the evolution of ourselves and the world. They would be places to stir the intellectual, social, and spiritual ferment needed for this quantum jump. Because a school does not exist at this time, we are like scattered shepherds, doing our best in separate locations with little ongoing association, shared teaching, or continuing collegiality. Although the Internet helps in the connections, and conferences and occasional convenings are vital, they are not stabilized. We need ongoing venues for the research and development of conscious evolution.

Education for conscious evolution will attract innovators in every field. Students will study the world as a whole system in transition from one phase of evolution to the next — identifying breakdowns and viewing problems as evolutionary drivers leading to innovation and transformation. Through their studies, the students' evolutionary vocations will be discovered and connected to people and projects that need their skills. We find out what we are really capable of in the context of the evolution of our species as a whole.

Resources for Conscious Evolution

But where will the resources come from to undertake this great enterprise? Which universities or foundations will call it into being?

I believe the leadership and resources will come from citizen leaders rather than from existing governmental or educational institutions. Tremendous resources are required to fully bring forth the potential for our spirit-motivated plan of action for the 21st century. Fortunately, there is a profound evolution occurring in the area of philanthropy that matches the needs of this initiatives. For example, *Forbes* magazine's cover story of May 1997 stated,

> America's two richest men, Microsoft founder William Henry Gates III, age 41, and Berkshire Hathaway chairman Warren Buffett, age 66, have set the new tone. Gates has said that of his estimated $18.5 billion net worth, he will give $10 million each to his baby daughter, Jennifer, and her future siblings, with the rest going to charity. Buffett has been less specific about how much his three children can expect, but has indicated they should not expect much.[4]

An example of cutting edge philanthropy occurred in 1997 when an anonymous family provided more than $30 million as the founding grant to establish the Institute for Civil Society, headed by Pam Solo. This was the first of perhaps $100 million in grants from one family to support what we are calling the social potential movement.

What finer place to position the cutting edge of philanthropy than on the frontiers of our progress, fostering the true wealth of nations? If one gives money to old institutions, the inherent tendency is to repattern the money into old forms, but the solutions needed for today cannot come from social architecture that is maintaining the existing systems. Breakthroughs by their nature need to break away from the current institutional structures. America, with its entrepreneurial nature, is a breakthrough society that takes risks, leaps of faith, and tangible actions required by this initiative.

A Program for Masters in Conscious Evolution

What follows here is a template for graduate study in the field of conscious evolution. It is ready to be developed, many faculty members are identified, and financial resources need to be found. The program will serve as a catalyst to launch the new field of conscious evolution and is for those who choose to be leaders of positive change in the 21st century. It will focus on the plan of action that emerges from this worldview and how we can contribute to it. Participants will bring a high level of mastery from many fields, accompanied by a deep calling to leverage their skills in vocations of social innovation and planetary change.

Education in conscious evolution builds upon students' knowledge and skill and their desire to enhance their vocational fields. For example, the same way a computer scientist at IBM might get a master's in business administration, professionals may choose a master's in conscious evolution to expand their understanding of how to manage their most valuable asset, themselves, thus gaining a broad, systemic understanding of where society is creating new opportunities for success.

The educational program has two concurrent themes: social evolution and self-evolution. Each theme is seen from its past, present, and future perspectives. These themes unfold concurrently, as represented in the diagram. They join at the apex of the triangle where social evolution and self-evolution converge in the work of building a cocreative society.

Education for conscious evolution is an integral part of the plan of action. What is being proposed here is an integrated set of actions, each of which is possible, plausible, and mutually reinforcing.

PROGRAM FOR MASTERS IN
CONSCIOUS EVOLUTION

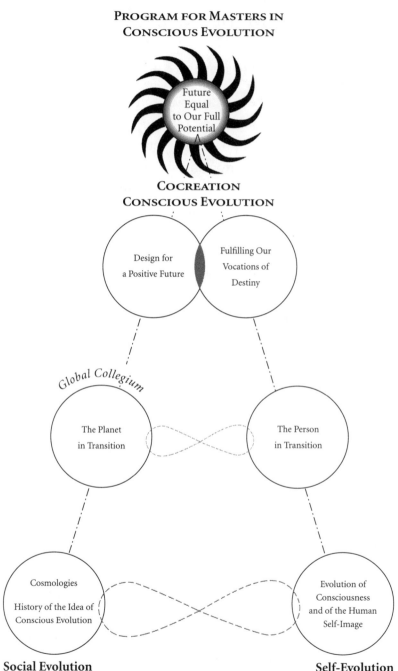

Future
Equal
to Our Full
Potential

COCREATION
CONSCIOUS EVOLUTION

Design for
a Positive Future

Fulfilling Our
Vocations of
Destiny

Global Collegium

The Planet
in Transition

The Person
in Transition

Cosmologies

History of the Idea of
Conscious Evolution

Evolution of
Consciousness
and of the Human
Self-Image

Social Evolution

Self-Evolution

THE FIRST COURSE

Social Evolution — Cosmogenesis

We begin by studying the past. In social evolution it is cosmogenesis — the history of the evolution of the universe from the big bang to us and beyond. We see the process as a continuous creation leading to us as cocreators. We learn from the laws and processes of evolution how to now guide evolution wisely. We study the work of Teilhard de Chardin, Ervin Laszlo, Beatrice Bruteau, Brian Swimme, Hazel Henderson, Jonas Salk, Abraham H. Maslow, Buckminster Fuller, Duane Elgin, Elisabet Sahtouris, Peter Russell, Eric Chaisson, Riane Eisler, Ken Wilber, and many other evolutionary thinkers and activists.[5]

We consciously place ourselves in the new story as we conceive and choose our future on the current turn on the spiral. We review the disciplines — geology, biology, anthropology, history, religion, science, psychology, art, current events, and future studies — as the unfolding process of creation in all its aspects: geogenesis, biogenesis, anthropogenesis, and more. By understanding evolution as the expression of universal intelligence, now becoming conscious of itself within us, and as us, we overcome the dichotomy between current evolutionists who see no design in evolution, and creationists who often propose an anthropomorphic God as creator.

The History of Conscious Evolution

Along with our study of cosmogenesis, we explore the history of the idea of conscious evolution. Transformationally motivated people are the growing edge of a great continuity of souls reaching back to the very earliest times. We must never think of ourselves as alternative, far out, or disconnected. We are in fact the growing tip of the greatest tradition of both nature and history. Remember, the nature of nature is to transform. Those who tend toward transformation are nature personified. And in human history there has been a continuous and growing impulse toward the regeneration and transformation of humanity.

Prof. Michael Grosso traced the faith that the deep and radical regeneration of human society is possible. Identifying the idea through Western history, he wrote in *The Millennium Myth: Love and Death at the End of Time,*

> It starts with the Babylonian Creation stories, the Hebrew prophets, Jesus, Paul, Joachim of Fiore, the Renaissance, the Enlightenment, the American Revolution, Boston Transcendentalism, through current visions of the end of this phase of evolution and the beginning of the next, springing from science fiction, New Age, general evolution theories, and technological innovators, [all seeking to participate consciously in the transformation of Homo sapiens, its metamorphosis into a species capable of life ever-evolving.]
>
> This core image is revealed in John's vision of a new heaven and a new earth, and in the closely related ideas that at the end of time the very laws of nature will undergo a vast overhauling in which it may even be possible to defeat death and once and for all liberate human society from injustice, from pain, and above all, from the curse of lovelessness.... *The Millennium Myth* taps into the totally unpredictable, creative rage of the human heart and imagination.[6]

The prophesies of end times of destruction of the old world order are intuitions and premonitions of the radical discontinuity from one stage of evolution to the next — which is happening now.

We are the latest expression of what may be the most fundamental impulse of human consciousness, which separates us from the animal world. Sometimes I look at my beautiful cat, Jack. He purrs, he sleeps, he eats, he hunts, he enjoys himself, but he doesn't try to be more than a cat or even a better cat. His cathood is established. But our humanhood is still incomplete. Conscious evolution embodies the great tradition of nature and of human aspiration. It is only now, however, that it has burst upon the scene as central to our survival.

Self-Evolution — The Evolution of Consciousness

This course, which also studies the past, focuses on the origin and evolution of consciousness itself, from the first cell to us and beyond. The work of Richard Maurice Bucke, M.D. in *Cosmic Consciousness* sets the stage for this study. He defined three forms of consciousness,

> (1) Simple Consciousness, which is possessed by the upper half of the animal kingdom ... (2) Self Consciousness, by virtue of which man becomes conscious of himself as a distinct entity apart from the rest of the universe ... (3) Cosmic Consciousness, a third form which is as far above Self Consciousness as is that above Simple Consciousness. The prime characteristic of Cosmic Consciousness is, as its name implies, a consciousness of the cosmos, that is the life and order of the universe — an intellectual enlightenment or illumination, which alone would place the individual on a new plane of existence. To this is added a state of moral exaltation, an indescribable feeling of elevation, elation, and joyousness, and a quickening of the moral sense, which is more important both to the individual and to the race than is the enhanced intellectual power. With these come what may be called a sense of immortality, a consciousness of eternal life, not a conviction that we shall have this, but the consciousness that we have it already.[7]

Bucke said that although cosmic consciousness was rare, it is now arising in many people through the natural tendency of evolution to create higher consciousness. Our goal is the stabilization of ourselves at the new norm. Students would experience the broadest variety of teachers and teaching to support them in moving toward this goal.

The Evolution of Our Self-Image

In this course we also reflect upon the evolution of self-image throughout history. Our self-image deeply affects our behavior. O.W. Markley wrote in "Human Consciousness in Transformation,"

> A variety of writing throughout history indicates that the underlying images held by a culture or a person have an enormous influence on the fate of the holder. No one knows the total potentiality of humankind, and our awareness of human "nature" is selective, shaped by our explicit and implicit images. In a provocative book, *The Image of the Future*,[8] the Dutch sociologist Fred Polak noted that when the dominant images of a culture are anticipatory, they "lead" social development and provide direction for social change. They have, as it were, a "magnetic pull" toward the future, by their attractiveness and legitimacy they reinforce each movement that takes society toward them, and they influence the social decisions that will bring them to realization. As a culture moves toward the achievement of goals inherent in its dominant images, the implications of the images are explored, progress is made, and needs are more fully satisfied.[9]

In this program we study the self-images humans have held in India, Greece, China, Israel, Christendom, the Renaissance, and the modern, existentialist, and post-modern eras to discover the effects of various self-images on human behavior and well-being. For example, imagine the different effects of the following beliefs:

- This life is merely a test for the next life.
- Whatever condition you are in, it is your fate or karma from past lives and there is nothing you can do to change it.
- There is no meaning to the universe, and your life is of no significance except what you give it.
- Everything you do counts forever. You are an expression of the whole process of creation; you are a cocreator.

What do we really want to be when we grow up? As memes or idea systems can be chosen for society, so too can our self-images be selected through intuition and alignment with our soul's purpose. The process of choosing a self-image can be guided only by accessing that soul purpose, that deeper calling, and surrendering to it. As we see ourselves, so we become. Students are charged with consciously creating self-images — higher-self portraits. Noetic technologies — the science of intellect — including the implicate processes of the mind such as intuition, reframing, and visioning are used.

THE SECOND COURSE

Social Evolution — The Planet in Transition

In the second course we study the present. In social evolution it is the study of our planet in transition. We have already seen the present as a period of our birth with all systems in transition. We have imagined a fully functioning innovations website. Our breakthroughs and innovations are connected. Our successes are communicated on the NewNews and through many outlets. The networks are networking. Innovators from every field often seen on the NewNews and other such media are becoming familiar newsmakers. All these activities are the living school of conscious evolution.

Students reconceptualize the planet as a whole system in transition from one phase of evolution to the next, recognizing our problems as evolutionary drivers and our breakthroughs as connected points of transformation that reveal the emerging civilization. These breakthroughs are the work of social innovators in all fields. They form the heart and soul of the curriculum for conscious evolution. Their way of living, their work, books, tapes, and projects are the basis of study. This ever-expanding group is on the Internet, increasing the synergy and interaction at the growing edge of positive change.

Students are invited to study the breakdown/breakthrough model of whole system transformation. They identify leading organizations that are mapping the suffering and destruction, such as Lester Brown's annual comprehensive compendium of negative trends for the World Watch Institute, the World Wildlife Fund, the Sierra Club, the Natural Resources Defense Council, Amnesty International, and the Human Rights Watch, to fully understand the nature of the problems we face. Then they seek out the points of transformation — the social innovations and solutions that are cropping up everywhere in relation to the problems. They study the work and the people who are changing the world. Whenever possible, leaders of positive change become mentors. As students become engaged in the mapping and mentoring process, their evolutionary vocations are stirred and it becomes easier for them to see what they really want to do in the world. (I can hardly imagine what this would have meant to me when I was a college student. It would have saved me at least 20 years.)

Self-Evolution — The Person in Transition

The second course in self-evolution corresponds to the second course in social evolution. In this course we study the person in transition. We apply the breakdown/breakthrough model to ourselves. We are each cells in the living body of the larger whole. Whatever is happening to us is both personal and part of the whole, just as every cell in our biological body is both unique and part of the body. Whatever we are going through is part of the planetary struggle to evolve. Our personal crises are also births of ourselves as members of the larger body. We do not do this work for ourselves alone.

In this course we ask ourselves, What in our lives is not working? What do we need to heal, mature, evolve? And what is working — what is breaking through? What are our peak experiences, our high-performance capacities? With this model we begin to design our self-development programs. Our spirituality, our creativity, our relationships and vocations are nurtured and encouraged. Evolutionary circles are formed to provide an environment of spiritual intimacy, nonjudgment, and safety to bring forth our full potential. Faculty guide and coach us to refine our programs. Then we commit to the practices required to achieve higher states of being. The evolution of society and self are inextricably interrelated and interdependent. Just as we encourage the social innovations that can bring society as a whole to a higher quality for all, so we encourage personal practices and principles of cocreation to evolve the individual, such as acceptance, affirmative prayer, community building, healing, nonviolence, synergy, meditation, networking, visioning. We are entering upon a lifelong path: the path of the cocreator, both social and personal.

Students are offered the best of modern teachers in every area:

spiritual growth, creativity, relationship, health, diet, and vocation. While studying those they most admire, plus doing inner work, students begin to embody their higher self-portraits. They create vivid descriptions of themselves in a flow state, early self-images of themselves as cocreators — universal humans. As we see ourselves, so we become. Our self-image becomes the basis of our personal course of self-development.

THE THIRD COURSE

Social Evolution — The Design for a Positive Future

Now we enter the convergence process together. Students, mentors, colleagues, innovators, and friends join in an extraordinary process of cocreation. Its purpose is to initiate an ongoing process to design a world that works for everyone. This design would be drawn from the study of social innovations working in every field and sector of the wheel.

One of the world's most creative social designers, Hazel Henderson, wrote in *The Politics of the Solar Age* about the need to redesign all our systems in the coming of a new era of enlightenment:

> A Solar Age is based on light-wave and solar technologies. In this Solar Age, we humans would engage in a bottom-to-top design revolution. The centralization of industrialism would give way to a new devolution: We would reshape our production, agriculture, architecture, academic disciplines, governments, and companies to align them with nature's productive processes in a new search for suitable, humane, and ecologically sustainable societies.[10]

As a complement to Hazel's focus on sustainability on Earth, Eric Drexler (one of the innovators of the radical new capacity called nanotechnology, the ability to build atom by atom, emulating nature itself) wrote in *The Engines of Creation,*

> Molecular assemblers will bring a revolution without parallel since the development of ribosomes, the primitive assemblers of the cell. The resulting nanotechnology can help life spread beyond Earth — a step without parallel since life spread beyond the seas. It can help mind emerge in machines — a step without parallel since mind emerged in primates. And it can let our minds renew and remake our bodies — a step without any parallel at all.... These revolutions will bring dangers and opportunities too vast for the human imagination to grasp.[11]

This is the design work for the positive future. It has never been done before, and it will never be finished. Students will be helping to form the future in the present. They will not be working with blue-sky visions or dreams, but with practical capacities already existing to build our field of dreams. Mentors in each sector of social change meet with students in a prolonged "design science revolution," as called for by Buckminster Fuller, Hazel Henderson, and others. Working on both the Internet and onsite, students and their mentors enter the ongoing process of codesigning futures based on what works.

Self-Evolution — Fulfilling Our Vocations of Destiny

Students pick areas of their choice and have opportunities to work on ideas, projects, and initiatives with people who are doing the work that excites them. This contact stimulates and deepens vocation. Through this process the participants' life purpose is enriched and fulfilled in an environment of excitement and discovery. The joy of learning is now expanded to include connecting our talents with meaningful work and wherever possible with people and projects to work with — the key to self-actualization. Remember Maslow's discovery: The key to self-actualization — a life of creativity and joy — is to find work that is intrinsically valuable and self-rewarding.

Although many current jobs are disappearing, the idea of work as creative expression is growing. In the new schools for conscious evolution, students discover the full meaning of vocational education. The education for conscious evolution elevates the concept of vocation to mean life purpose in the service of self and society. Liberal arts are vital to help us understand and envision what we choose to create, just as all other branches of learning become essential instruments in our evolution.

Schools for conscious evolution help fulfill our great drive for self-expression — self-actualization through meaningful work and chosen life purpose. They become magnets not only for current cultural creatives, but for the far larger number of incipient evolutionaries — imaginal cells in waiting. When this field is established, it will draw to it those ready to participate in the evolution of self and society. I imagine this would be a majority of the young and many of us seeking vocations that excite us — at whatever age.

Visions of a Cocreative Society

At the apex of our program is the yet mysterious cocreative society, the next stage of human evolution. Out of education in conscious evolution there emerges an intuitive and intellectual understanding of the quantum transformation. The societal butterfly is revealed in all its glory.

Visions of our future will be developed, cultivated, dramatized, and communicated to the ever-growing community of cocreators. The magnetic field of our collective potential will draw us forward to realize it. When we build the field of our dreams, we, humanity, will come to fulfill ourselves. When there is no vision, people perish. When there is vision, people flourish.

PART IV

THE GREAT AWAKENING

CHAPTER FIFTEEN

The Great Awakening

The world is ready for the advent of a new stage of human consciousness and action. It is time for an initial collective awakening, an experience of shared empathy. We might call it a planetary birth experience. Preparations are being made by millions of people as they make their plans for the year 2000. (See Part 5: A Call to Action on websites.)

Ken Carey wrote in *The Third Millennium,*

A mother never knows exactly what hour she will give birth to her child, but she has a "due date," an approximate time when the baby is expected and will most likely be born. For millennia now there have been those in various traditions of both East and West who have known that the earth has a due date sometime during the second decade of the 21st century. Though there will be much awakening of individuals prior to the first unified movement of the awakened planetary organism, this movement, like a first breath, will occur in but a single moment.[1]

Such a planetary awakening could happen now because the timing is right in relationship to our planetary life cycle. Let's continue with our biological analogy. A newborn baby awakens at a specific time in its life cycle, just after it has made its journey from the comfort of the womb into the harsh and strange world. The child finally rests at peace. At one delightful moment, which cannot be predicted yet is expected, the infant awakens, relaxes, opens eyes that have never seen — eyes that were created in the darkness of the womb. For the first time the womb-veil thins, light floods in, the infant focuses and sees its mother. A radiant glow of recognition and joy crosses its face and animates its body. It has come home to the new world, never to go back again.

Let's compare ourselves as a planetary organism to the biological organism just after birth. We are the generation who is alive just after the birth of this planetary body. We are the ones facing the trauma just after birth — struggling to coordinate ourselves as one global system. We are shifting from our mother Earth's nonrenewable resources to renewable sources of energy and nourishment. We are learning to handle our waste, to stop overpopulating and polluting. And we are beginning to recognize that we are all members of one planetary body.

For the first time — in the 1960s — we opened our Earth-bound eyes, saw ourselves from outer space, and fell in love with ourselves as a whole. For one brief moment we saw no boundaries, no nations, and no walls to divide us.

Now, millions of us are awakening to our participation in the whole, as the planetary body integrates and links up throughout the world. Our electronic media have joined us via global satellite. More recently, the Internet, our refined planetary nervous system, is connecting us as individuals and groups, cross signaling through the system, beyond the confines of time and space.

Let's imagine that the new function of the Internet is to inform us of what is now working to evolve our world. Let's assume that the NewNews in all its forms is communicating to us the news of who we are becoming. The plan is unfolding. But we are still in a postnatal torpor, traumatized and confused by the abruptness of the changes we are undergoing. Many of us are without hope, without the sense that our future is desirable and attractive, forgetting that each of us has a part to play. Yet, as Teilhard de Chardin writes in *The Future of Man*, "The whole future of the Earth, as of religion, seems to me to depend on the awakening of our faith in the future."[2] We live with an ominous sense of impending doom, which is realistic. If we do not quickly adjust to our new condition, we may die. Our birth could be a death. The dangers we face are life threatening, just as the newborn infant faces critical problems that must be quickly handled or it will die.

Something more is needed to awaken us as a whole — an infusion of life, love, appreciation, and security to comfort us in our time of trial. It is this event that we now envision and that we can in fact bring into being. Remember, everything that rises, converges. The planetary dissipative structure is reaching maximum instability. Everything we do counts, especially in this critical time. Will the impulses of health and creativity prevail soon enough to counter the acceleration toward environmental and social breakdown?

A Planetary Birth Day Celebration

What is needed to facilitate the positive shift is a catalytic event that would connect us spiritually, emotionally, and practically; an event with such a powerful impact that the global state of mind would forever be changed; an event so inspiring that the world would never again doubt that we have the capacity and the will to make it, that everyone on Earth has a chance to survive and grow, that each of us is needed, and that all of us are part of the universal creative process. We might call this event a Planetary Birth Day celebration. We have had two great Earth Days to awaken us to our environmental crisis. This, however, would be the first Planetary Birth Day. It would awaken us to our creativity, our love, and our potential for life ever evolving.

The event envisioned would be a 24-hour celebration, a complete Earth Day for our Birth Day, in the model of the great Live Aid global satellite broadcast in 1985, which linked more than 2 billion people for 18 hours on the theme of hunger. Our Planetary Birth Day would link as many, if not more, for a 24-hour celebration of the creative potential of humanity in the Third Millennium.

Elements of the Great Awakening

Let's imagine how the great awakening — our Planetary Birth Day — is celebrated. The first element is spiritual. Everyone who prays, meditates, or contemplates is asked to do so during the event. We have prepared for this element during many world healing and world peace days. Countless people are already linking up in meditation across the planet. On our Planetary Birth Day, everyone is asked to participate at the same time, and our goal is to have at least 1 percent of the human race involved. One percent of 5 $^1/_2$ billion people is approximately 55 million people. This is possible in today's globally connected world. During this day people from every religion, culture, and tradition are aligning their thoughts and prayers on humanity's potential for goodness and creativity.

Prayers and meditations are communicated via all media from all regions of the world. Poems of praise for the potential of humanity are heard around the word. Forgiveness is offered and received as groups everywhere pray that the illusion of separation be dissolved and ask for forgiveness for the pain we have inflicted upon one another, upon other species, and upon Earth herself.

The second element is emotional; it touches the heart. Musicians perform live from all parts of the world — an expanded Live Aid — playing their indigenous music in celebration of humanity's potential. The music arouses our love and compassion. We feel empathy toward one another, expanding beyond family, tribe, and nation to embrace the world. We feel the excitement and expansion that often bursts forth in large parades and celebrations and during great sports events.

From every part of Earth, original music is heard. Imagine that Joseph Eger, conductor of the United Nations Symphony Orchestra, is conducting a planetary concert. All kinds of music interweave until we hear one planetary beat, one musical heartbeat pulsating rhythmically throughout Earth. It entrances and aligns our hearts and minds. One sound that can be hummed and sung in every tongue emerges from the planetary symphony. It is the note of D flat, known as the tone of Earth. It is the vibration that has been measured coming forth from healers in the act of healing. People attune to the tone. Brain waves and heartbeats synchronize. Tensions ease, intuitions rise, love is felt as a palpable opening of the heart.

The third great element in the celebration begins: the practical. The moment comes when from every region and culture social innovators and creators link up via the Internet. The NewNews broadcasts loud and clear from all over the world pragmatic and caring voices saying to the planetary child, "We can feed, we can house, we can educate, we can restore, we can explore, we can cooperate, we can cocreate." For we are already doing it! Vignettes of successful projects are communicated via global satellite, just as instances of overcoming hunger were communicated during Live Aid, interspersed with the song "We are the world, we are the children." The combination of prayers, music, and demonstrations causes a new awareness to course through the minds of billions of people simultaneously. The hosts of the event show the trends that these innovations can lead to, inviting artists, poets, and dancers to celebrate their visions of what humanity can become when we grow up.

As the event continues the media audience grows. As we saw in the movie *Network*, people start opening their windows and instead of saying "We won't take it anymore," they are shouting "We're going to make it! We have a future!"

Let your imagination soar now and see that people begin to gather in the streets, malls, churches, temples, mosques, in the bush and fields, in cities, towns, and villages. When the Berlin Wall came down people joined in joyful celebration of their liberation. Now thousands of Berlin Walls begin to come down — the walls within our hearts that hold back the pent-up love dammed by our illusion of separation and our fear of one another. Not only do we remember that Earth has no physical boundaries or borders, but also we now feel in our hearts that we are not divided against one another by false stereotypes, labels, and customs. We feel an uprising of love and forgiveness.

We have had many intimations of this experience: We felt it during VJ Day when the war with Japan was over. I was in an apartment in New York City when the announcement came. I heard a roar from the city as people opened their windows and cried out with joy. People flooded into the streets. An irresistible tide of relief and celebration brought people into each other's arms. Strangers were hugging and kissing with abandon. I went into the street and was carried away by the enthusiasm of the crowd.

We felt it again when Neil Armstrong set foot on the moon. Bells rang throughout the world. We identified ourselves as the people of Earth on a new world. We saw glimpses of such outpouring in the "Reach Out and Touch" ceremonies at the 1984 Olympics, when people in the stadium were asked to reach out and touch people from all nations and backgrounds. As I watched the feelings mount, I knew that a sense of joining wanted to spill out of the stadium, that the millions watching on television wanted to reach out also. But we were isolated in our separate homes.

It happened again during Live Aid. It happens during the yearly World Healing Mediations, and on Earth Day; it happens whenever two or more of us are joined together in our love for Earth, for one another, and for Spirit.

Now, at long last it can happen for our Planetary Birth Day on a scale that has never happened because the time is right: the media are available, our planetary nervous system is ready to link up, the Internet has already connected the new capacities of the social body, our prayers have aligned our thoughts, and the music has opened our hearts.

The planetary beat quickens as the planetary song spreads. The tone, the sound, the beat, the breath, the song reverberates in human consciousness as the reassuring voices of the builders of the new world convince us that we can survive and grow. We are going to live. We *do* have a desirable future, and everyone is needed.

Then comes that moment, that due date, long awaited. A silence descends upon Earth. The love we feel for one another, for nature, and for Spirit, however we understand it, unites us. We open our eyes together. A smile of joy courses through the planetary nervous system — our first planetary smile. In that instant we are a united humanity. We open our eyes together and see the light of who we really are. We are all part of one global family with the capacity to care for all our members. We are ready to discover the vast and unknown potential of an awakened humanity. We can never again forget who we are.

Many efforts are moving in this direction. For example, I recently attended an extraordinary conference of 200 religious and spiritual leaders hosted by the United Religions Initiative. This group is an effort to stop the violence among religions and foster peace in the world by offering a space for continuing dialog and connection among the religions. A proposal was made that there be a 2-day event held December 31, 1999 and January 1, 2000. The first day would promote a cease-fire among all religious combatants throughout the world. The second day would be a celebration of humanity's creativity and compassion. Peace-building initiatives in all fields would be joined and demonstrated amidst prayer, meditation, music, and drama.

It is just possible that this group, joining with other comparable efforts, will effect such a great awakening. It is a natural potential in a system awaiting such catalytic action.

We can imagine that following such a celebration, just as the religions would continue their interactions, teams of social innovators would come together in a continuous process of cocreation. The new social architecture for cocreation would be visible. We would then have experienced both the alignment of loving consciousness and the increased interaction among innovating elements, broadcast worldwide via all media. The patterns that connect us would be strengthened. Millions would be aroused to join in the effort to grow and nurture a new world.

Concurrently, the United Nations creates the first Peace Room, as sophisticated as a war room. It is connected to comparable sites in nations and regions of the world. Let's imagine that the Peace Room is inaugurated on the annual World Peace Day. One of its facilitators is Robert Muller, former assistant secretary general of the U.N. who helps to preside over the greatest coordination of the positive the world has seen. In a global ceremony we dedicate the Third Millennium as the 1,000 years that have been given to us for the evolution of our species. Dr. Muller declares that we are to become a universal humanity, coevolutionary with nature and cocreative with Spirit. We are at a new beginning. The great awakening has happened. The 21st century has come. We have made it through the crisis of our birth without further violence.

CHAPTER SIXTEEN

The Cocreative Society Revealed

The cocreative society was seen by visionaries and seers of all cultures, envisioned as heaven on Earth, the new Jerusalem, Paradise, the Promised Land. In some deep sense we all know it, for it has been told to us since time immemorial. It is ourselves fulfilled. Now we see that this new state of being is not life after death, but life at the next turn of the evolutionary spiral.

Reviewing Our New Story

To envision the cocreative society, we review our new story — the story of the emergence of universal humanity and of the individual cocreator maturing in the fullness of time, when the noosphere is ripening, when we have increasing abundance, access to knowledge, personal freedom, and an unprecedented ability to choose our own destinies.

The cocreative society occurs when this superorganism, this noosphere, this immense collective power of modern society is consciously and lovingly oriented toward the evolution of humanity. It is the result of our awakening to our capacity to restore Earth, to free ourselves from poverty and disease, to further emancipate individual creativity, to develop synergistic social and economic systems, and to convert our military-industrial-technological complex to the restoration, protection, and enhancement of life on Earth, and the exploration and development of outer space.

The cocreative society cannot be imposed or engineered into existence. It is nurtured into being by increasing the connections and coherence among those already initiating vital actions. It emerges when we collectively overcome the illusion of separation that has divided us, for the capacities we need — the technology, resources, and know-how — are already present in their early stages to realize our evolutionary agenda. Only a catalytic spark of shared love and spiritual experience is needed to activate the great genius of humanity to join in inspired actions. The great awakening is a vision of such a catalytic event.

The cocreative society may seem impossibly difficult from the historical perspective, but from the evolutionary perspective we are encouraged. Imagine early humans, shivering in caves with nothing to protect them from the weather, starvation, and animals far stronger and quicker, being told that one day they would have to protect other species and care for nature herself. Imagine the pioneers seeing for the first time the Pacific Ocean and being asked to envision today's Los Angeles. Since all that happened, we cannot doubt that the next step is possible, and indeed, inherent in the nature of reality.

A Preview of Coming Attractions

In our movie of creation, we allow ourselves to see ahead and to feel what it is like to be at the next stage of our evolution. Let us now stand together in the future-present and welcome ourselves. Let's take the quantum jump and preview the coming attractions.

Our purpose here is to use our intuition and see our future based on potentials now awakening within us, so that we can propel ourselves forward to fulfill our destiny. Our intuition is not based on mere dreaming, but rather on our deepest intentions, choices, and known, as well as, emerging capacities. We are going forward now to imagine what it will be like when everything we know we can do, works.

To cocreate this image of a positive future, we connect peaks of human performance and exceptional ability, from mountaintop to mountaintop. Let's draw an imaginary line from peak to peak and establish a new plateau of excellence and creativity based on the best we can do in all fields. Let's awaken our memory of the future and feel what it is like when we are whole, healthy, and normal beyond the illusion of our separation. When there is vision people flourish, grow, emancipate, and create that which they desire.

This vision of the future is my intuition and heart's desire. It is what I choose. It is what I stand for. As you read, consider your choices, your deepest longing for a future, not in the immediate moment, but perhaps 500 years hence, when we are in the next stage of evolution. What do you see when you imagine our highest creativity connected and established as a new normalcy?

What It May Be Like

Let's lift ourselves for a moment beyond the blue cocoon of Earth. Penetrating the vastness of the universe, floating in weightlessness as our astronauts do, we see a few frames ahead in our movie of creation. We are becoming fully human. Our cosmic consciousness is stabilized. We experience infinitely expanding awareness, deeper and deeper interrelatedness. The veil of matter has disappeared. Reality is more like a thought than a thing. Empathy increases and intentionally expands.

We make direct contact with the evolving core of the spiral — with universal intelligence. The designing process that is forever creating the universe breaks into our awareness as we begin to cocreate on a planetary scale. As mentioned previously, centuries ago great religious avatars came to this planet in a state of cosmic consciousness — the Indian seers, Akhenaton, Moses, Buddha, Jesus, Mohammed. They sensed themselves as directly connected with Source. All taught an ethic of love, a faith in the process of creation, and a promise of life beyond the body of the individual and the planet.

Few ordinary people could share their experience, so religions, dogmas, and institutions formed to hold the promise. Now, because of the natural rise of consciousness and freedom, millions are experiencing direct personal contact with a deeper reality. Spiritual connection with Source, or the metapattern, becomes the norm and is stabilized because a critical mass has achieved it. Mass resonance reinforces it, and the nervous system of the social body, our mass media, is communicating stories of people who are in that state as the norm. Every day we hear what we can do that is good. We begin now to catch a glimpse of the glory of our full potential self — universal humanity growing up.

We gain continuity of consciousness with all dimensions of reality in an eternal present, a nonlocal field of all possibilities out of which everything is always evolving, as the great avatars have always demonstrated. Our awareness incorporates both the eternal and the evolving aspect of God. We are able to maintain our eternal oneness — the still center — while creating, as the creative intelligence does, in space and time.

The genius that built us from a fertilized egg to a human being is our genius. We are that which we know. We gain knowledge by identity. We are the creative genius of our own body-minds. The secrets of the atomic, molecular, and cellular worlds are revealed to us when we are at one with the process of creation through internal awareness as well as through scientific investigation. Conscious evolution ultimately means that the cosmic intelligence that is manifest in every particle and entity in the universe becomes self-aware in us, as us. The separation of the rational mind from the great creative process dissolves, and we recognize that intelligence as our own. With that intelligence, we create as we think. Descartes' dictum "I think therefore I am" becomes "I think therefore it is." Our thoughts are translated ever more directly into manifestation.

We have shifted from what Gary Zukav called in *The Seat of the Soul*, the five-sensory human to the multisensory human.[1] We are naturally aware of multiple dimensions of reality. Our isolation from the spiritual world, or other dimensions, is overcome through our expanded knowing of the full spectrum of reality.

We discover there is a library of consciousness recorded in a great memory bank of what Ervin Laszlo called the "vacuum-based holofield" and the "cosmic Internet" in his book *The Whispering Pond*.[2] He hypothesized that there may be a physical medium, the vacuum-based holofield, that is self-remembering and is able to hand down the characteristics of the parent universe (universes that came before ours) to our offspring universe. That is how the great yogis can see past lives. It is all there. Nothing is lost, not a hair, not a feather. While the physical universe is increasing in disorder the intelligence of the universe is increasing in order and coherence. Everything is recorded in the mind of the cosmos, is remembered, and is ultimately available to those in cosmic consciousness. Everything we do, experience, and think remains available. We discover that the universe is increasing in creativity, intelligence, and coherence, as are we. We realize that the direction of evolution is for the universe with its billions and billions of galaxies to become conscious of itself as a whole. This is the fulfilled vision that Eric Chaisson foresaw in *The Life Era.*

We cultivate higher states of being, here and now. Out-of-body experiences, telepathy, clairvoyance, psychokinesis — all the dormant extended capacities that were embodied in the great yogis, avatars, and founders of world religions become the norm. We can do the work that Jesus and others did, and even greater works, for we are now born into the superorganism. We find that our metanormal capacities, as Michael Murphy said in *The Future of the Body*, are normal for universal humans.[3] We are democratizing the miraculous as the next stage of our evolution. Our higher spiritual and personal capacities, now combined and integrated with the electronic and extended capacities of the social and technological body, are a quantum jump as great as from the earliest human to us.

The Illusion of Separation Is Overcome

As cosmic consciousness stabilizes in a critical mass, it becomes more difficult to maintain the illusion of separateness. Because millions of imaginal cells are already moving in that direction and because we have imagined that we have already established a shared resonant field of this awareness through the first planetary birth experience, it is more natural for individuals to reside in the expanded state as a new norm.

The near-fatal human flaw of consciousness — the illusion that we are separate from one another, from nature, and from Spirit — is healed through the mass resonance and the emergence of millions of imaginal cells who tend toward universal, holistic consciousness. The great human problem of evil stems from the illusion of separateness. Whenever this illusion is overcome, we behave lovingly to one another. In the gentle birth, the separated mind is consumed in love. The violence that has been foreseen in Armageddon-like scenarios is avoided. A gentle planetary birth is achieved. The separated mind cannot stand apart from that field of love. When enough of us hold together, the gentle birth is facilitated.

As the illusion of separation dissolves, we see that we can coordinate ourselves naturally as one body. As love pours forth from our hearts, the larger body of universal humanity is unbounded, free at last to reveal its magnificent and beneficent collective creativity. It becomes obvious that we are all members of one body. New economic, social, educational, environmental, and political systems naturally emerge out of this consciousness. What seems (and is) impossible in self-centered consciousness is natural and normal in cosmic, whole-centered consciousness.

We Enter the Global Brain

We now have become fully connected to the global intelligence system. We are active participants in the global brain. We ask for information and receive it from the collective memory bank of the larger body, just as we now ask ourselves to find a memory and images of that experience appear on our mental screens.

Our larger global brain functions as an extended nervous system and brain for each of us. On the inner plane we are nonlocal — we are part of the one mind. On the outer plane, through our global brain, we are also nonlocal and omnipresent, accessing all information instantly, as needed.

There is a mechanical aspect to everything that has form, but our global brain is more than a machine: it is an extension of our own brain. We have integrated our extended capacities gracefully and no longer feel separated from our larger body. Future extensions of computers, phones, faxes, radios, and televisions are simply used as extensions of ourselves. As Jerome Clayton Glenn wrote in *Future Mind: Artificial Intelligence: Merging the Mystical and the Technological in the 21st Century*, "Through Conscious Technology, civilization will evolve into a continuum of technology and humanity...." [4]

We Become Self-Healing and Self-Regenerating

As we stabilize our universal consciousness and connection to Source, we become self-healing and self-regenerating beings. Our healing arts — prayer, meditation, visualization, exercise, diet, and loving care — integrate with our magnificent medical advances. We understand the language of our bodies. We resonate with and unlock the inner secrets of our body-minds.

As our consciousness grows, our bodies no longer seem like strange creatures we do not understand and bring like separate objects — a lung, a liver, a finger, a heart — to doctors to be examined under a microscope like foreign bodies. We know our bodies. We have within us what Deepak Chopra called the "great cornucopia of healing substances." [5] We become intimate with our own bodily genius and integrate the wisdom of our hearts with our intellectual understanding of how nature works. We heal and regenerate and eventually evolve our bodies by conscious choice.

We learn thereby to extend our lives by choice and to end our lives by choice. Remember, evolution raises consciousness and freedom with every turn of the spiral. We now enter the third life cycle. The first cycle began with single cells who were semi-immortal and divided to reproduce themselves. The second cycle began with multicellular life that evolved sexual reproduction and scheduled death of the individuals, as parents learned to degenerate and die. The origin and diversity of the species began. The third cycle begins when we hit the limits to growth on the planet and begin the shift from procreation to cocreation. We learn to give birth by choice, to die by choice, and to extend our lives by choice.

In the third cycle, life extension and conscious dying emerge naturally. Those who have more to create choose to live on until they are finished with their work. When we feel that our creativity has run its course, we gracefully choose to die. In fact, it seems unethical and foolish to live on. The stereotype of aging changes. People are regenerated through their creativity to live as long as the creation calls them. When we are old and tired of life and do not want to live on, we learn to die by choice, as some native people do. The sorry picture of millions of people bent with age, wishing to pass on, with nothing to do, nowhere to go, no possibility of renewal seems barbaric and cruel in retrospect.

It is my preference that, when I feel complete with this life, I call in my beloveds, my family, my friends. In a momentous celebration I will prepare to enter the mystery of the next phase of life and seek the blessings of those I love. I choose to make my transition gracefully.

Sexual reproduction and scheduled death evolved millions of years ago. In the third cycle they evolve once again, this time toward conscious reproduction, conscious life extension, and conscious dying. The mammalian life cycle becomes the universal life cycle. We are the generation on the cusp of this great transition. We feel it even now: increased sensitivity to the power of thought, belief, and attitude in achieving optimum wellness and even rejuvenation.

We continue to transform from the current human to the cocreative human spiritually and physically as well. As Eric Drexler said in *Engines of Creation*, quoted earlier, that nanotechnology can "let our minds renew and remake our bodies."[6] When we combine our cosmic consciousness with our capacities to transform our bodies through both healing and medical advances, in an Earth-space or universal environment, we realize that the emergence of universal humanity is not a metaphor, it is a fact. As real as the evolution from *Homo neanderthal* to *Homo sapiens* is the jump from *Homo sapiens* to *Homo universalis*.

Eventually, as we learn to live beyond our planet — in the solar system and among the galaxies — we find that our bodies are not appropriate for long-distance travel. We learn to design bodies that are viable for universal life. This need may well be the long-range meaning of our new capacities such as cloning or bioengineering. Our purpose is not to redesign our bodies for life on a crowded planet, but to consciously evolve our bodies for life beyond our planet. We are crossing the great divide from creature to cocreator physically, mentally, and spiritually. Nature always creates new bodies for new frontiers; witness the sequence of bodies from fish to amphibians to mammals to humans, and now to universal humans. We are at the threshold of genuine newness. The only difference between us and other creatures who experienced a radical change is that we are entering the process consciously.

From one stage of evolution, the next stage tends to look like a miracle. How would a bird look to a single cell? How does universal humanity with its godlike powers look to us? Everything is miraculous, this step no more than the rest. Why, having seen the miracle of our emergence from sub-atomic particles, would we be surprised at our next step of evolution?

Chosen Children

In the next phase of our evolution, we have chosen children. Contra-ception has become pro-ception. Parenting is a vocation, not a necessity or an accident. Not all people will choose to have children, but those who choose do it consciously and whole heartedly. Each child is a loving act of creation. Each child is chosen, welcomed, needed, and beloved. He or she is recognized as a vital member of the social body.

Education for conscious evolution is available everywhere. It is the process of discovering each child's creative expression, cultivating it as the most precious resource on Earth, and connecting it with the people and tasks where it can best flower.

Schools open their doors — they take down their walls and release our children to become cocreators of new worlds. The needs of the world are the schools' lifelong curriculum. Everyone is a teacher to someone and everyone is a student of someone. Each child is on a quest to discover his or her purpose, gifts, and work in participation with the evolution of the larger body. Students and mentors are busy throughout the educational systems codesigning the new world, seeking the synergies among all the parts.

The Cocreative Couple

Men and women join as coequal cocreators in the society of universal humans. The purpose of their holy union is to give birth to each other as cocreators and when ready, if so choosing, to give birth to the chosen child. Each child born in the new society is welcomed as a universal human.

This shift in relationship is fundamental to planetary transformation. As women have fewer children and live longer lives, their loving creativity is rising — an irresistible tide of desire to express and find life purpose in the world. This drive is eventually as powerful as the drive to reproduce. It is the suprasexual drive to evolve ourselves. Now we become the cocreative couple, which begins when both partners achieve within themselves at least the beginning of a balance between the masculine and feminine, the animus and the anima. It begins when the woman's initiative and vocational need is received in love by the feminine receptivity of her partner. When she is loved for her more masculine side, she falls in love with the man's feminine aspect, for what she needs is the nurturance of her own strength and creativity. She loves him for his receptivity. He no longer has to prove himself by control and domination. He can bring forth his own creativity without aggression. And she can express her strength without fear of losing him. Whole being joins with whole being, recreating the family at the next stage of evolution. Same-sex couples experience a similar process of integration and joining to emancipate each other.

The breakup of the 20th century procreative family structure is a vital perturbation needed for the breakthrough of the 21st century cocreative family structure. The cocreative couple forms the basic family unit of the cocreative society, neither matriarchy nor patriarchy, but partnership, laying the foundations for the next stage of democracy, for synocracy.

Synocracy Emerges

Individualistic democracy evolves into "synocracy," or synergistic democracy. Freedom comes to mean the ability to fully express our uniqueness as vital members of the whole community. Win-lose voting develops into win-win-win decision making — how to achieve a win for both parties and for the community and environment as a whole. Because the whole is always greater than the sum of its parts, we discover that by cocreating rather than by competing each individual and group can better achieve its fulfillment, for there is more for all. Although there is always competition to stimulate excellence, the emphasis is for each member of society to achieve his or her full potential within the whole.

Robert's Rules of Order, which was such a great advance over killing one another, becomes Synergistic Rules of Order, a win-win-win process that takes into account the interdependence of life and seeks to find a way for the self-interest of each party to be achieved so that it complements rather than defeats the self-interest of others. Remember, our more unitive consciousness has been secured. We are not trying to solve our problems in the same state of consciousness in which we created them.

Government evolves from its coercive, bureaucratic phase to its new role as coordinator and facilitator of people's creativity. Genuine self-government is achieved as people become truly self-governing — that is, higher-self governing.

The vast kindergarten of humankind formerly served by the police, the welfare system, mental hospitals, and prisons gradually grows up. The problems we faced in the 20th century are not solved; they are dissolved, as the problems of a 2-year old do not exist for a 20-year old.

We have no desire to overpopulate, for most people are experiencing the joys of cocreation, extended life and an ever-expanding sense of participation in the whole. The military-industrial-technological complex is challenged to work for the restoration of Earth, and the genuine protection of people from terrorism and planetary disasters while it gains tremendous capacities from space exploration and development. Resources now locked in the military and in social services, which generally serve a still-immature humanity, are freed for the tasks of the evolutionary agenda. Their tasks of new world building, both on Earth and in outer space, are suitable to their highest self-images and more noble aspirations, which have been distorted by past systems of competition, and there is genuine profit to be made in environmental restoration, socially responsible business, and space development. James Redfield lays forth such visions of the future in *The Tenth Insight* and *The Celestine Vision*.[7]

The Hierarchy of Social Needs has been accepted. The vast resources and brilliance of our species are now focused on the evolutionary agenda rather than on overconsumption, excessive competition, and aggressive defense.

We still have problems, but they won't be the same ones. Our current issues of hunger, poverty, war, ignorance, greed, and injustice are all symptoms of our sense of separation from one another, from nature, and from Spirit. After we mature in our spiritual, social, and technological abilities, we find that we do know how to make the world a physical success without damage to the environment or jeopardizing anyone.

The problems we will face are really unimaginable to a newly born universal humanity. Remember, we are born into a universe of billions and billions of galaxies, some of which may have life comparable to our own. We have not yet met other life in a verifiable way. Perhaps we must evolve through our own maturation before we can meet others.

Our growth potential is immeasurable. We saw our faint beginnings as we watched the Mars Pathfinder land July 4, 1997. It dropped upon Mars' rocky terrain, bouncing in its balloon-like covering, until it settled and opened itself like the egg of a baby turtle. Then it deflated its covering, opened its petals, turned on its camera eyes, and prepared to crawl out! It began immediately to photograph rocks and send the pictures to Earth. It took 8 minutes for the signals to go to and from Earth, so the Pathfinder was programmed with rules. It knew what to do when confronting a boulder or a precipice. One scientist said that the Pathfinder had the intelligence of a bug. He went on to say on television, "People of Earth, you are the soul of the Pathfinder. It is your eyes, your hands that touch the rocky soil of a new world."

And so we begin the process of bringing inanimate matter to life. Soon we learn to bring life to planets and to build little habitats in space using nonterrestrial materials and solar energy. We become an Earth/Space, or solar system, people. We are preparing for our life as a universal humanity.

Earth becomes a new world as we build new worlds in space. It is our natural and cultural home, to be loved, enhanced, and conserved in harmony with other species. The wilderness, however, is no longer on Earth; it is in the vastness of the universe, the genuine unknown. As once long ago life crept out of the seas onto the barren planet, we now reach beyond our mother Earth to establish our extended home. When the sun completes its life cycle and burns all its planets, we will be star children, a galactic species. Memories of our Earthbound life will be reconstructed as we now piece together the story of the origin of life on Earth.

Few of us can conceive of the new potentials we shall discover as we take the next step as a universal species. The benefits of exploring and developing our full range of human potential in a universal environment will lead to options inconceivable to a self-centered, Earthbound species.

We have been gestating in the womb of Earth. We may be surrounded by other life forms, but unable to see or feel them because we have been limited in our awareness. The universe is unitary: its laws are the same throughout, its chemistry consistent. If we do meet other life, although we may be physically diverse, what we will all be increasingly conscious of is the One Source from which we all come.

On the inner plane, we emerge as beings in the image of that creative intelligence that so many call God. We are godlike in our power, we are universal, and we participate in the evolution of matter itself into consciousness and life. We recognize in all humility that we are an infinitesimal part of an infinite universe, capable even in our infancy of resonating with that infinity to an ever more precise degree.

A Vision of the Future:
A Fulfillment of the Aspirations of the Past

We are one body, all people. We coordinate as a planetary body, attuning to one another and to the designing intelligence.

We are immortal. We are not bound by the limits of the body.

We are universal. We are higher beings. Our innate sense of growth potential, our intimation of a higher state of being is true.

We are conscious cocreators, partners with God. Mystical and secular awareness unite in evolutionary consciousness as we attune to the pattern in the process and assume some responsibility for the technologies of creation.

The future affirms the past. The root of "religion" is *re-ligare*, to bind back and make whole. We are reunited with our entire evolutionary past — from our cosmic conception through our birth into the universe.

We are in contact with other life. The intimations of higher beings is affirmed. We have always been in contact intuitively. The esoteric or hidden is becoming exoteric and clear. Once we saw through a glass darkly. Now we see face to face.

We know more about the creative process. We know more of the laws of the universe as we become more creative and powerful. The laws that guide us are the laws of evolutionary process and transformation. The precedent we draw upon is 15 billion years of success. As infinitesimal cocreators we greet the infinite universe with the humility of hope that we are loved, we are good, we are needed, and we are capable.

The separation is over. Through expanded love and knowledge, the desire for deeper union with the creative intelligence, God, is satisfied.

We become the second couple at the second tree — the Tree of Life. Adam and Eve were symbolically the first couple. They joined the masculine and feminine together and made a whole being, wherein they reached the Tree of the Knowledge of Good and Evil, and separated from the animal world. To reach the Tree of Life, to have access to the powers of creation, each person must become whole, uniting the masculine and feminine, the yang and the yin, the rational and the intuitive. Then we can unite whole being with whole being, cocreator with cocreator. The second couple reaches the second tree, the Tree of Life, the tree of the healing of the nations. Cosmic consciousness is secured.

We see that the meaning of our crisis is to activate our new capacities. The purpose of our new powers is universal life. Universal humanity is born, is alive, is well, and is growing. Our birth has been accomplished. We are at a new beginning.[8]

Participating in the Quantum Change

This vast vision of the next stage of our evolution may at first seem beyond us. What can anyone do as an individual, in a whole system transformation of this order, when often it seems hard to get through the day? Our participation in the quantum change starts at home, in our personal lives, in that infinitesimal yet momentous flick of a decision to say yes to our unique potential. The quantum transformation unfolds through our joining with one another in small groups to stabilize our higher consciousness and to affirm our higher qualities of being — evolutionary circles of all kinds to birth the universal human that each of us is. The quantum transformation continues as we discover our callings, our chosen vocations. Each life purpose is a vital element in the emerging body of humanity. As we nurture the seeds of our unique genius, we commit to growing them in the world. We form our teams and partnerships; we select initiatives to carry our life purpose into manifestation at the growing edge of change. These projects become our progeny, our offspring — they are loving expressions of our combined genius. Our commitment carries us forward to bring the inner work of personal and spiritual growth into spirit-motivated action in the world. The human potential movement grows into the social potential movement. Each of us is a seed of transformation in the social body. As we connect with one another, imaginal cell with imaginal cell, we design new social systems, innovations that bring forth the essential goodness and creativity of others. Through these social innovations, the outline of the new world emerges in vivid and brilliant colors, alive with creativity and diversity. An ever-evolving blueprint for a positive future is revealed in the countless acts of excellence and love now evolving our world.

We enter a period of lifelong learning while reaching out through our colleagues, organizations, and media to communicate the NewNews. We find that whatever age we are chronologically, we are very young from the point of view of our chosen work.

Cocreators are all in the early stages of the new human archetype, gaining resources, skills, and know-how in the great task of repatterning and cocreating a world. As the larger system builds up its perturbations and instabilities, our infinitesimal positive steps tend increasingly to connect and converge.

Through this speeded up interaction of innovating elements, society appears to repattern itself — a dissipative structure moving to greater complexity. The change may seem to be a sudden quantum jump, but it is actually the fruit of the long, laborious, dedicated work of millions of souls, known and unknown, who like ourselves have been called from within to express their life purpose in service to the world. The larger metapattern joins us into a new whole, different from and far greater than the sum of our parts. The societal butterfly appears replete with greater freedom, consciousness, and synergistic order — glorious beyond the imagination of the individuals who have composed it.

To Take a Stand

The purpose of *Conscious Evolution: Awakening the Power of Our Social Potential* is to discover a peaceful passageway through the labyrinth of modern society, to carry us from here to there, to unearth a design of evolution for a gentle birth, and to formulate a spirit-motivated plan of action to cooperate with the tendency in evolution for higher consciousness and greater freedom through more complex or synergistic order.

Is this plan possible? It depends on you and me.

I remember during my vice-presidential campaign when I visited Joan Holmes in her office in New York City, she told me of the origins of the Hunger Project, which takes a stand for the sustainable end of world hunger.

"Who started this?" I asked.

"I did," she said. "I took a stand that there would be no more hunger."

I was amazed. At first she took the stand alone. Each of us at some point in our lives takes a stand alone. But the moment we do, we find we are surrounded by others who have also taken a stand. Even if our intention doesn't seem to have been fully realized, the collective impact of our choices is moving us forward in the right direction.

I take a stand for the gentle transition of humanity toward a future equal to our full potential. I join all others taking such a stand. Together we are a mighty force.

When asked what I choose to be the outcome of the book, my answer is that it serve the fulfillment of the plan.

"May Light and Love and Power restore the plan on Earth." That is my prayer.

PART V

A CALL TO ACTION

WHAT WE CAN DO NOW

The emerging field of conscious evolution is now calling forth the most innovative understanding concerning the next step in human and planetary development. The field is potentially an umbrella for all disciplines and activities that assist in the maturing of our species, offering a place in consciousness to discover and enact positive visions of human future.

The Foundation for Conscious Evolution, a nonprofit educational organization, was formed in 1991 to serve this growing new field. Our vision is that the foundation will become a point of focus and orientation for humanity's immense journey of conscious evolution — one of many new planetary places for the convergence of wisdom — ancient and modern, scientific and spiritual — to be understood, synthesized, and harmonized into a matrix of evolutionary intent.

In its first phase the foundation has worked to bring conscious evolution into form through my books, lectures, tapes, an experimental school for conscious evolution, and the cocreation website (see Resources Section).

As of this writing the Foundation offers four steps you can take to participate in the process of conscious evolution. These are vital ways to enter the spirit-motivated plan of action for the 21st century by activating your own purpose and passion to create. Together they offer an introduction to the curriculum in conscious evolution. These steps are:

- *Evolutionary Circles* for personal and spiritual growth.
- *The Rings of Empowerment* to help you discover your vocation and manifest it in the world.
- *SYNCON,* a process of synergistic convergence to help bring your organization, business, or community together as a whole in such a way that members are further empowered to achieve their life purpose in cocreation with others.
- *The Cocreation Website,* a place to enter your projects, to find your teammates, and to learn from golden innovations now transforming our society, keeping you updated on events, insights, materials, and products, and NewNews in our domain of awareness.

Evolutionary Circles

The first step in the process is to form an evolutionary circle, for clearly, the path of the cocreator is not followed alone. By its nature it requires community and communion with like-minded friends. The path is activated when we join together in a field of resonance and affirmation to support one another in self-evolution and in making our contribution to the world.

The circles are a structured program showing how we can overlay the evolutionary perspective into our lives. Their purpose is to establish an environment of spiritual intimacy, safety, and nonjudgment in which to give birth to each full potential self. Circles are composed of two or more friends who agree to meet regularly for about 2 $^1/_2$ hours for at least 12 weeks. The circle process can be introduced into existing support groups or can be used to begin one.

The first hour is dedicated to the inner spiritual inquiry and begins with a series of questions: Where am I now on my spiritual journey? Where am I off the mark? Where do I need to forgive and be forgiven? What are the qualities I now affirm in myself that are most vital to my evolution? These questions are offered in a supportive environment and act as a potent stimulus for each person until the next meeting. In the second hour participants listen to audiotapes and evoke their own ideas in a cocreative dialog that calls forth the intuitive knowing. The circle can be a self-organizing seminary, a seedbed for the emergence of the universal human, and a way to ground these ideas in our daily lives.

An evolutionary circle album is available to guide you through the process. The album includes a guidebook showing how to form a circle, a reading list for your study, a videotape of the evolutionary spiral, and four 1-hour audiotapes that set forth seven steps on the path of the cocreator: cocreative spirituality, the cocreative person, cocreative relationships, vocations, community, society, and how we can form a larger community of conscious evolution through e-mail and gatherings.

The Rings of Empowerment

The second vital step is to discover and manifest our life purpose in creative action. *The Rings of Empowerment* is an excellent manual for those who wish to form vocational core groups and teams. It is designed to help you practice the principles of cocreation in finding and actualizing your life purpose in the world. It takes you from the inner work of personal growth into the outer work of the social potential movement. It is an excellent next step after evolutionary circles.

The Rings are a map of what works in small groups and cocreative teams. I discovered them during my vice-presidential campaign when I visited positive future centers and noted what people were doing to center and strengthen themselves as they reached out into their communities. Then, in cooperation with Carolyn Anderson and Global Family, a nonprofit educational organization dedicated to networking and supporting people in becoming members of one global family, we developed this manual. Global Family offers core group training that illuminates each of the rings.

These practices occur spontaneously whenever great teamwork is found. We have studied what has worked and have mapped a wide range of processes. When all are practiced concurrently and consciously by a team, quantum change occurs. The manual is a guide through this process. Each ring is a practice that leads to the empowerment of yourself and your teammates. The following is a brief outline of each ring, which is further developed in the manual.

Ring 1: Activating the Cocreative Self

The rings begin when one person takes a stand and commits to bringing forth his or her full potential self in action in the world.

Ring 2: Connecting at the Heart

After we have claimed our desire to realize our deeper vocation in the world, it is natural and necessary to find others who have an affinity for our purpose. The next ring occurs when one person decides to form a group to fulfill a vocation or to further discover a life purpose. We reach out to find others who share our passion and are excited by our dreams. We learn to cultivate resonance, echoing one another's highest intentions.

RING 3: LOVING ONE ANOTHER AS OURSELVES

The next step is love. The environment in which resonance is nurtured, expanded, and fulfilled is love, acceptance, trust, forgiveness, and nonjudgment. The moment judgment or criticism enters the group, resonance is lost and the heart connection that feels so good is temporarily broken. Love is more demanding than resonance. In this ring we practice the Golden Rule — loving one another as ourselves, minute by minute, every day, in our workplaces, homes, and activities of all kinds.

RING 4: COMMUNICATING OUR INSPIRED INSIGHTS

The cocreative person synthesizes the best of the rational and intuitive mind. In this ring we practice cultivating and expressing our intuition directly in cocreative dialog. We learn to establish an environment of silence to listen for the inner voice, to speak directly as our intuitive selves, and to allow the "still small voice of God" within to be heard and to guide our actions.

RING 5: SECURING OUR CONNECTIONS THROUGH CEREMONY

In this ring we develop ceremonies to help us anchor and actualize the state of resonance and acceptance. We consciously make our relationships and our workplaces sacred. Music, silence, prayer, affirmation, vision quests, and appreciative inquiries belong in this ring and bring the team to a higher degree of excellence and respect for one another.

RING 6: COCOACHING ONE ANOTHER
TO DO AND BE OUR BEST

In this ring we learn to become a great team. Each of us has an image of our higher self, even if dim. It is the butterfly within the caterpillar. In cocoaching, the first step is to assist one another in seeing ourselves at our highest, as imaginal cells becoming magnificent cocreators. Then we learn to coach, not criticize, such that all members of the team are supported in doing and being their best.

RING 7: DISCOVERING OUR LIFE PURPOSE

Here we move from the inner work of personal growth to the outer work in the world. The human potential movement within us becomes the social potential movement. If the ring process is guided by a leader who already has a life purpose, then the teammates have joined around his or her dream. But for the process to work, the life purpose of each member needs to be activated by the chosen task. It does not work if a group is merely helping someone else succeed. Synergy is achieved when members of a group become more actualized through cooperation in the whole. Therefore, it is necessary to help each person further identify his or her vocation within the work at hand. A vocation is not a destination; it is a path through which to fulfill our destinies. We learn to model the change we seek in the world by being the change ourselves.

RING 8: RELEASING THE DECISION —
DISCOVERING THE DESIGN

How do we make decisions as cocreators? In this ring we explore the path of right action by combining our intuition with our logical minds. We learn to put all the facts on the table and then call on our deeper knowing to reveal the implicate design. We seek win-win solutions as members of one body. We practice sapiential authority — the one who knows best has the most authority. The best and most natural place to practice right human relationships and synergistic decision making is in the small group — in our work and our families.

Ring 9: Committing to Shared Purpose Through Joint Action

Some groups already have a joint project and want to practice the inner rings for greater harmony. Others do not yet know what they want to do and need to seek their vocations. The rings help in both cases. Often at this stage the core group reassembles based on actual commitment to chosen work. In this ring, the group formally chooses and commits to a specific project that helps each member more fully realize his or her life purpose.

Ring 10: Cocreating Through Cooperative Entrepreneurship

In this ring we learn the best of business skills combined with social purpose and the commitment to the growth of each team member. We attempt to carry resonance, love, and inspired insights into the world through our work. Here the separation between the inner work and the outer work dissolves. Our work is our spiritual path, and our spiritual path is our work. Our avocation and our vocation become one. We seek the next level of economic freedom — the freedom to earn our living by doing the work we love with those who most attract us for the good of ourselves and our world.

SYNCON (SYNergistic CONvening)

SYNCON is the next stage of the democratic process — a way of bringing all members of a group, organization, or community together to discover how each person's passion to create can be supported, connected, and fulfilled through participation in the whole community. SYNCON works with groups from twenty-five to several hundred people. The process is very simple.

1. People meet in each sector of the wheel according to their functional interests and vocational calling. (The wheel categories discussed in this book may be used or others devised as needed.) Participants form one or more circles in each sector of the wheel. A scribe, a facilitator, and a spokesperson volunteer.

2. Each member of the circle responds to three questions:
   • What is my passion to create now?
   • To fulfill this desire, what do I need that I do not now have — what is lacking?
   • What resources do I have to give to this group or to people in other sectors of the social body?

3. After listening carefully to one another, participants form smaller groups based on shared purpose and affinity. They support one another and often devise joint plans.

4. The smaller groups reassemble in their sector of the wheel and share their joint strategies.

5. Each sector prepares a composite statement of goals, needs, and resources.

6. The whole group meets in an Assembly of the Whole. The assembly can be visually exciting, in theater-in-the-round style, with ribbon dividers, placards, or artistic renditions to suggest the different functions of the social body.

7. Each task force spokesperson presents the shared statement of goals, needs, and resources of its group to the assembly. Everyone listens actively to each presentation, noting where one group's needs and another's resources match. "Vocational ambassadors" are assigned by the group to visit other sectors.

8. A facilitated mingle occurs, either of functional sectors or of individuals and groups, seeking the synergies, linkages, and connections that are natural to any system, but are often unnoticed because the process does not facilitate their discovery. If a video camera is available, it becomes the "nervous system" of the group. People call for the camera whenever they have a breakthrough or new linkage. The Four Ss — synergy, syntony, synchronicity, and suprasex — are cultivated. If possible, a NewNews show is edited from the event, expressing the fact that cocreating is the news now, fostering the social uprising of wellness.

9. The Assembly of the Whole reassembles. Each group represents its goals, needs, and resources, taking into account expanded connections and synergies. According to the time available, the assembly can discover more synergies and experience the fact that the whole is greater than the sum of its parts. Nature forms whole systems out of separate parts, as we have seen. When these parts connect in a nonlinear, exponential interaction, a quantum jump may occur. We discover in SYNCON that the energy of the whole is greater than the sum of its separate members. Participants find they are better able to achieve their goals through cocreation than through adversarial or even competitive tactics. Music and dance can be used. In the end, a celebration occurs and people walk the evolutionary spiral together.

10. Each task force is invited to place its goals, needs and resources on the Cocreation website. Eventually, when the system is developed, the website will help find common goals and match needs with resources throughout the system. People can check golden innovations in their fields to serve as inspirations and guidelines for newly emerging projects.

We recently had a SYNCON on Kauai, in Hawaii, sponsored by Women of Vision and Action. The former mayor, who had been in office during the hurricane that almost destroyed the island 5 years ago, participated. She said that her people did not want to grow as a commercial venture and were forming a "spiritual vision of a new civilization on Kauai." They had the vision, the people, the ideas, but they lacked the process. "SYNCON is the process we have been seeking," she said. A woman from Israel told us that the dialog between the Palestinians and the Israelis had broken down. They had to move beyond conflict resolution. She invited us to bring the SYNCON to Israel. Elisabet Sahtouris, the great student of how natural systems evolve, stood and said, "Let's have a SYNCON in the Temple of Epidaurus in Greece in the year 2000 to celebrate global democracy."

A SYNCON manual and training is in preparation as of this writing.

The Cocreation Website

The Cocreation website, in its first phase, allows individuals and organizations working in the field of social innovations to post their projects in one of four stages of development: vision, startup initiatives, projects that are working successfully, and golden innovations — projects now successfully transforming a system in the social body. Projects are categorized according to the eight major sectors of the innovations wheel. Individuals and organizations may search the database in these categories to find teammates and resources. They are also allowed to edit, update, or delete their projects. A specially designed collection form asks key questions (including the questions asked at the SYNCON) so that individuals and groups can match needs and resources and learn from the successes of others.

A beginning global collegium of social innovators is also posted with current thoughts and links to the innovators' websites. The collegium is open-ended and will continually grow. Also on the website is a comprehensive library consisting of seminal works for further study and a current events section posting workshops, gatherings, and NewNews updates.

Lectures, teachings, products, books, tapes, trainings, and events in conscious evolution are also available. For further information on the Foundation for Conscious Evolution, the Evolutionary Circles, the Rings of Empowerment, the SYNCON process, the Cocreation website, and the books, tapes, lectures, and events of Barbara Marx Hubbard, contact:

Foundation for Conscious Evolution
P.O. Box 6397
San Rafael, CA 94903-0397
Tel: (415) 454-8191
Fax: (415) 454-8805
E-mail: fce@peaceroom.org
Website: http://www.cocreation.org

RESOURCES

Vital Initiatives For Conscious Evolution

Everywhere throughout society remarkable initiatives are evolving our world. The activies listed in this chapter are a microcosm of the planetary transformation in every sector of the wheel. As you read through them, imagine what it would be like to bring together these and other such activities in a synergistic process — to connect, cooperate, and cocreate. Each would be linked to many others. We would find ourselves, I believe, living through a social quantum jump, a repatterning of our society as a dissipative structure in transition to the next order of complexity, freedom, and consciousness.

The groups selected are ones I know personally, some few of which I have cofounded and am actively cocreating with. Most weave through many sectors and functions — they are hybrids. Some have been mentioned in this book. Others are noted here for the first time. This list is by no means complete. Some are established; others are new and fragile.

As you read, notice which you are attracted to, which excite your passion to create. If you feel so moved, join in, meet other pioneering souls, and find your larger role within the quantum transformation now at hand. Or, create a new activity of your own and call others to join you.

As you participate, you literally grow wealthy, for real wealth is measured in cocreative relationships that inspire us and foster life-long learning and companionship toward the evolutionary agenda.

Governance and Law

Governance as used here is broadly defined as the effort to bring transformational values into the organization and development of democracy. These efforts transcend left, right, or center; they move us forward and upward. They are part of a third way, which seeks the best from the full spectrum of initiatives with emphasis on the flowering of the complete human within a regenerative planetary-universal culture. Moving beyond ideology into a new pragmatism, those involved in the evolution of governance are working toward a win-win, cooperative, spiritually-based, socially and economically just democracy.

THE CENTER FOR VISIONARY LEADERSHIP
3408 WISCONSIN AVENUE N.W., SUITE 200
WASHINGTON, D.C. 20016
TEL: (202) 237-2800; FAX: (202) 237-1339
E-MAIL: CVLDU@NETRAIL.NET
WEBSITE: HTTP://WWW.VISIONARYLEAD.ORG

Corinne McLaughlin and Gordon Davidson have founded The Center for Visionary Leadership in Washington D.C. Their educational path included residency at Findhorn, the spiritual community in Scotland, and then forming their own community in

Massachusetts. In true pioneering fashion, they reach out to the socially responsible business world as well as to leading edge political transformative agents from both parties in Washington. The center is a point of transformation in the nation's capital, attracting a wide variety of leaders. It provides spiritual insights and innovative, whole-systems solutions to social problems. It offers public programs, consulting, and values-based leadership training to meet the needs of a wide variety of individuals and organizations. Courses in nondenominational spiritual development are featured as well as citizen dialog to help heal the issues that divide us as a nation. It brings political and spiritual leaders together to find ethical principles for solving social problems. You are welcome to participate in lectures, classes, and trainings offered. Currently, the center facilitates a dialog on spiritual politics. Participants include major leaders in spiritual development, and government, writers, the media, and business pioneers. Corinne and Gordon's book *Spiritual Politics* is an important guide.[1]

THE CAMPAIGN FOR WHAT WORKS
E-MAIL: EMLECAIN@AOL.COM

Eleanor LeCain directs *The Campaign for What Works*, an effort to catalyze the overall social potential movement and lead toward a new politics in the United States that will liberate our creative potential. As of this writing, Eleanor is advising Marianne Williamson on a short- and long-term strategy for holistic politics. Eleanor was the long-range planner for Massachusetts through the Blue Print 2000. She is now considering running for the state senate in Massachusetts and is working on her forthcoming book, *What's Working in America*.[2]

THE FOUNDATION FOR ETHICS AND MEANING
26 FELL STREET
SAN FRANCISCO, CA 94103
TEL: (415) 575-1200; FAX: (415) 575-1434

Michael Lerner, author of *The Politics of Meaning*, has founded the Foundation for Ethics and Meaning as a vehicle to build a movement to change the bottom line in American society, to shift the paradigm from selfishness and cynicism to caring and solidarity.[3] His foundation has built local chapters around the country; some are now exploring initiatives to require state and local governments to consider a corporation's history of social responsibility before awarding government contracts.

THE MENTOR CENTER
27331 OAK KNOLL DRIVE
BONITA SPRINGS, FL 34134
TEL: (941) 947-1708; FAX: (941) 947-2670

The Mentor Center, currently being founded by Beverly Lieberman, will go beyond quick fixes and theory-based trainings to assure that those who have responded to their highest calling and have recently committed to a path of social leadership succeed over the long term. In times past, when people wanted to master a new skill or craft, they studied with an experienced mentor. Beginners learned by doing, the fastest and best way to learn anything. The center has been designed as a school for social organizers using a mentorship educational model. It is the purpose of the institute to inspire, train, and provide ongoing support to social organizers everywhere in actualizing their noble, humanitarian goals. Students will be matched with several appropriate, professionally trained expert mentors from social organizations, business, education, law, finance, marketing, the media, and government. They will work together to solve real challenges faced by people trying to change the old ways to new ways that reflect more love, more compassion, and more reverence for all life.

THE STATE OF THE WORLD FORUM
JAMES GARRISON, PRESIDENT
BOX 29434, THE PRESIDIO
SAN FRANCISCO, CA 94129
TEL: (415) 561-2345; FAX: (415) 561-2323
E-MAIL: FORUM@WORLDFORUM.ORG
WEBSITE: HTTP://WWW.WORLDFORUM.ORG

Jim Garrison, working with Mikhail Gorbachev, has founded The State of the World Forum in San Francisco. Each year an extraordinary array of political, social, cultural, scientific, and business leaders, including heads of state, meet to examine how to move toward a new civilization — a global society. A powerful network of initiatives has emerged, with forums now spreading to other regions of the world.

PATHWAYS TO PEACE
P.O. BOX 1057
LARKSPUR, CA 94977
FAX: (415) 925-0500; E-MAIL: PATHWAYS@IGC.APC.ORG

Avon Mattison's Pathways to Peace has initiated a five-year inquiry into peace building for the 21st century, in partnership with the Institute of Noetic Science and the Fetzer Institute, bringing together many distinguished leaders to examine soul-infused initiatives that lead to cultures of peace.

RE-CREATION: THE FOUNDATION FOR PERSONAL
GROWTH AND SPIRITUAL UNDERSTANDING
POSTAL DRAWER 3475
CENTRAL POINT, OR 97502
TEL: (541) 734-7222; FAX: (541) 734-2311
E-MAIL: RECREATING@AOL.COM
WEBSITE: HTTP://WWW.CONVERSATIONSWITHGOD.ORG

Neale Donald Walsch, author of *Conversations with God, Book I* and
II has started this foundation.[4] Its goal is to sponsor and produce
the first International Symposium on the Integration of Spirituality
and Governance. Neale believes that if we ever decided to govern
ourselves from the place of our highest spiritual understanding
rather than from our lowest thoughts and deepest fears, the world
could change overnight. Neale plans to host a symposium in 2000 in
collaboration with the Center for Visionary Leadership.

ACTION COALITION FOR GLOBAL CHANGE
LOLA KRISTOF
2101 SACRAMENTO STREET, APT 301
SAN FRANCISCO, CA 94109
TEL: (415) 922-6721; FAX: (415) 567-9522

This coalition proposes to make San Francisco a model city for the
21st century. Its mission is to work with all segments of the city,
including governmental, educational, business, social, cultural, religious, and environmental, to coalesce as one entity with the express
purpose of moving the city toward the stated objective while developing a prosperity from which all citizens will benefit. It will hold
town hall meetings, open forums, dialogs, round table discussions,
and brainstorming sessions to make this a true community project.
Lola Kristof, the directing force behind the model city project, wants

to create a site for a Peace Room, a place to continually scan for, map, connect, and communicate what is working in San Francisco.

THE FOUNDATION FOR GLOBAL COMMUNITY
222 HIGH STREET
PALO ALTO, CA 94301
WEBSITE: HTTP://WWW.GLOBALCOMMUNITY.ORG

The foundation's work spans half a century, involving individual spiritual growth, social action, grassroots education, and mediation of international conflicts (best known for work as Beyond War). Courses, lectures, development of educational videos, and publication of the bimonthly magazine *Timeline* are its current work.

Education

Education for conscious evolution, as we have seen, is growing in countless separate initiatives. All have the same intent — to bring forth the creativity of the individual in meaningful work that evolves the person and the world. Now we need to come together in some sort of consortium, to codesign a curriculum for the conscious evolution of humanity. The groups listed are vital elements of such curriculum.

WOMEN OF VISION AND ACTION
ROBIN GUETH
P. O. BOX 1746
SEDONA, AZ 86339-1746
TEL: (800) 909-9682

Women of Vision and Action is a remarkable network of women from all backgrounds who understand the urgent need for profound social change and commit their lives and actions to creating it. It was founded by Rama Vernon. The group integrates vision and action, spiritual values and social ideals. Its members and their projects seek innovative solutions for key challenges in local, national, and world communities and encourages women to join in mind, heart, and spirit to bring their visions into being. It is developing a leadership institute to educate women in transformational leadership. It offers regional conferences, joint initiatives, global linkup days, salons, circles, and gatherings, and publishes the *WOVA Network News*. Members use a wheel of transformation to identify and connect their projects and social innovations in their communities. The motto is: "Be the Change You'd Like to See in the World." A Men of Vision group is in formation.

SOCIETY FOR THE UNIVERSAL HUMAN
29500 GRAHAMS FERRY ROAD
WILSONVILLE, OREGON 97070
TEL: (800) 893-1000; E-MAIL: INFO@LECWORLD.ORG
WEBSITE: HTTP://WWW.LECWORLD.ORG

Rev. Mary Manin Morrissey is spiritual director of The Living Enrichment Center in Wilsonville, Oregon, which serves thousands of people in the principles and practices of cocreation. In January 1995 she invited several teachers to design a spiritual curriculum for the 21st century. She asked each of us to "teach at our own growing edge." Jean Houston, Gary Zukav, Gay and Kathlyn Hendricks, Joan Borysenko, Father Leo Booth, Mary, and myself met for several days, facing the question of what it was we wanted to do. We searched for a new form. It wasn't an institute, a university, or a center. We realized it was a society. The Society is in its formative stage and welcomes your participation in helping to create something that goes beyond the many conferences, networks, and associations. The goal is to become the ground out of which the microcosm of a new society of, for, and by universal humans can be nurtured and through which we can teach and learn from one another. The Society's events occur at the beautiful Namaste Retreat Center at the Living Enrichment Center, where Mary has a garden designed with nine paths to represent all the world religions, and one unnamed to represent that which is still to come.

UNIVERSAL HUMAN GATHERINGS
GARY ZUKAV AND LINDA FRANCIS
P.O. BOX 1333
MT. SHASTA, CA 96067
TEL: (800) 454-7685; E-MAIL: HEALING@SNOWCREST.NET

Gary Zukav and his spiritual partner, Linda Francis, offer extraordinary retreats at Mt. Shasta, California, and elsewhere to celebrate the universal human and to create family and community among us. During these retreats the barriers that separate us dissolve as we learn to tell the truth about how we feel with love for one another. In these events Gary places his own life in the laboratory of conscious evolution. Gary and Linda offer us an education for the heart and the soul of the cocreator. The retreats are participatory, experiential, and draw from Gary's books *The Seat of the Soul,* and his forthcoming *Universal Human.* [5]

JEAN HOUSTON'S MYSTERY SCHOOLS
P.O. BOX 3300
POMONA, NY 10970
TEL: (914) 354-4965
WEBSITE: HTTP://WWW.WAKING.COM/MYST_SCHOOL.HTML

Dr. Jean Houston is one of the great teachers and social artists of our generation and her mystery schools train thousands to see themselves as cocreators. She uses myths and historic figures as guides on the journey to wholeness. She has written many books, the most recent: *A Passion for the Possible: A Guide to Realizing Your True Potential.*[6]

WORLD CORE CURRICULUM NEWSLETTER
6005 ROYAL OAK DRIVE
ARLINGTON, TX 76016
TEL: (817) 654 1018; FAX: (817) 654-1028

BARBARA GAUGHEN MULLER
MEDIA 21, GAUGHEN PUBLIC RELATIONS
226 EAST CANON PERDIDO, SUITE E
SANTA BARBARA, CA 93101
TEL: (805) 968-8567; FAX: (805) 968-5747
E-MAIL: BARBARA@RAIN.ORG
WEBSITE: HTTP://WWW.WORLDPEACE2000.ORG/IDEAS

Dr. Robert Muller, former assistant secretary-general of the United Nations and chancellor of the University for Peace in Costa Rica, has formed the World Core Curriculum, which he says is the product of the United Nations — the global metaorganism of human and planetary evolution.[7] The curriculum provides the basis for a global education focusing on our planetary home, the human family, human groupings, our place in time, and the miracle of individual life. The curriculum has been translated into Spanish, Russian, Italian, Dutch, and German. Groups and individuals are using the curriculum in the United States, the United Kingdom, India, Canada, Australia, New Zealand, and the Philippines.

BECOMING A PRACTICAL MYSTIC
JACQUELYN SMALL
950 ROADRUNNER RD.
AUSTIN, TX 78746

Jacquelyn Small offers training and retreats in transformational processes for professionals and others seeking knowledge and experience of self-evolution.[8] With her co-leader, Don Gill, she teaches a mystery school entitled Becoming a Practical Mystic, based on the hermetic Western mystery traditions.

PROF. A. HARRIS STONE
LEARNING COLLABORATIVE
SACRED HEART UNIVERSITY
PARK AVENUE
FAIRFIELD, CT 06432
TEL: (203) 365-7514
E-MAIL: STONE@SCSU.CTSTATEU.EDU

Prof. A. Harris Stone has developed the Learning Collaborative in Connecticut with participating universities, including Sacred Heart and Southern Connecticut State University, where he is leading pioneering research in WHOLEfield Learning, developing transdisciplinary programs with a unique variety of academic people who are escaping from the academy. They are finding each other in the transdisciplinary context established by the collaborative.

NEW HORIZONS FOR LEARNING
P.O. BOX 15329
SEATTLE, WA 98115-0329
TEL: (206) 547-7936
E-MAIL: BUILDING@NEWHORIZONS.ORG
WEBSITE: HTTP://WWW.NEWHORIZONS.ORG

Dee Dickinson is identifying and communicating new educational and societal advances for the next century, including survival skills for our children's future. Her website is a breakthrough in clarity and usefulness, covering all areas of advanced educational initiatives.

OLIVER W. MARKLEY
PROFESSOR OF HUMAN SCIENCES AND
STUDIES OF THE FUTURE
INSTITUTE FOR FUTURES RESEARCH AT THE
UNIVERSITY OF HOUSTON
CLEAR LAKE, TX 77565
TEL: (713) 526-2214

Professor Markley is a pioneer with a master's degree in Studies of the Future at the University of Houston, Clear Lake. His most popular course was Visionary Futures — an exploration into altered states of consciousness and depth intuition, as described in "Using Depth Intuition in Creative Problem-Solving and Strategic Innovation" (selection 40 in *A Source Book for Creative Problem-Solving: A Fifty-Year Digest of Proven Innovation Process*).[9] His current course is Preparing for the 21st Century: Visioning for Successful Implementation. He has just written a most important article entitled "The Fourth Wave — A Normative Forecast for Space Ship Earth."[10] He is combining a deepening of the implicate order through noetic or consciousness technologies with a concurrent advance in the "explicate order" through nanotechnology. This is precisely the quantum jump we have foreseen when we combine our cosmic consciousnesses with our advanced technologies.

AUDREY COHEN COLLEGE
75 VARICK STREET
NEW YORK, NY 10013
(800) 33-THINK (84465)
OUTSIDE METRO AREA (212) 343-1234, EXT 5001
FAX (212) 343-8470

Audrey Cohen College, where scholarship is leadership, offers a "person centered system of education" with three semesters a year, in which a bachelor's degree can be earned in just 2 years and 8 months and a master's in 1 year. The system integrates career with studies. It is an education that assists students with participating fully in meaningful work in the 21st century.

CALIFORNIA INSTITUTE OF INTEGRAL STUDIES
9 PETER YORKE WAY
SAN FRANCISCO, CA 94109
TEL: (415) 674-5500

This institute is an accredited school of higher learning that emphasizes the integral perspective — nondualism, holism, and evolution; it focuses on completeness rather than on fragmentation and on the unity of polarities such as mind-body, human-universe, and masculine-feminine. It includes comparative and cross-cultural studies in philosophy, religion, psychology, organization and business, health, learning theory, and the arts. With the exception of the B.A. Completion Program, all students admitted to degree programs must have completed a bachelor's degree. Many courses and workshops are scheduled for evenings and weekends to accommodate the needs of working professionals.

JIM CHANNON, CONSULTANT
P.O. BOX 130
HAWI, HI 96719

Jim Channon, former lieutenant colonel in the U.S. Army, founder of the First Earth Battalion and the Natural Guard when he was in the Army, is now working on the concept of a planetary commons. In a private conversation, he said to me, "No one is paid to take care of the commons. What we need is a five-year moratorium for all our armed forces worldwide. There are no major external threats to any of today's nations. Each branch of the service would respectively take care of a portion of the planetary commons: air and space (air force), water (navy and marines), ground, soil, and fresh water (army). This work comes under the umbrella of natural security. The military has the systems, the values, the training, the organization, the purpose. The only thing left to fight over in the future is scarcity of resources. By attacking that problem up front, through preserving our resources and developing new ones, the military would still be engaged in real defense. Once they experience their new mission, they would never go back to the old ways, because the old ways do not work."

Jim is a consultant to many corporations, organizations, and communities.

BAKER PARK RETREAT CENTER
DAVID ELLIS
13179 BAKER PARK RD.
RAPID CITY, SD 57702
TEL: (800) 335-9938; FAX: (605) 343-7553

Into the dynamic new field of education for conscious evolution come people such as David Ellis. His work is representative of a new profession designed to tune us up, to work with us as individuals so we can participate fully as cocreators. David, author of *Becoming a Master Student,* which has sold more than 2 million copies, as well as *Creating Your Future,* and *Human Being,* has just created a think tank, a "sacred place in which to invent our futures."[11] He has built a physical facility in the Black Hills of South Dakota on the spiritual grounds of the Lakota Souix, where people can take the time to look toward and invent our multidecade and multisensory futures.

Economics, Business, Philanthropy

The evolution of economics works toward a socially responsible, sustainable, and regenerative system that can provide economic justice and abundance through meaningful work for all. Its purpose is to overcome scarcity and free up human creativity.

SOCIAL VENTURE NETWORK
P.O. BOX 29221
PRESIDIO BUILDING 1016, 3RD FLOOR
LINCOLN BOULEVARD AND TORNEY AVE.
SAN FRANCISCO, CA 94129-0221
TEL: (415) 561-6501; FAX: (415) 561-6435
KIM CRANSTON, PRESIDENT; E-MAIL: CRANSTON@WELL.COM
MARK DONOHUE, MEMBERSHIP COMMITTEE
E-MAIL: MTDONOHUE@AOL.COM

This network was founded in 1987. Its mission is to be part of an international community of business and social entrepreneurs dedicated to changing the way the world does business. The network is an invitational organization of business leaders who are senior executives or founders of socially responsible enterprises with more than $3 million in annual revenue, executive directors of progressive foundations with assets exceeding $20 million, or individuals or corporations of substantial net worth with a commitment to socially responsible investment. The goal of network members is to develop themselves personally and professionally so they can effectively advance long-term commercial activity that integrates the values of a just and sustainable society into day-to-day business practices. They provide a supportive environment in which they challenge themselves to envision and implement ways their enterprises can improve the world.

BUSINESSES FOR SOCIAL RESPONSIBILITY
1850 M STREET, N.W., SUITE 750
WASHINGTON, D.C. 20036
TEL: (202) 872-5206; FAX: (202) 872-5227

Businesses for Social Responsibility, cofounded by the Social Venture Network in 1992, is a sister organization. The group is an all-inclusive chamber of commerce for the progressive or socially responsible business movement and companies that are simply exploring what this means in relation to their organizations, which currently may not embody many socially responsible values. Its mission: "To meet the twin challenge of uniting the fast-growing number of socially responsible business in an alliance to shape government policy, the business environment, and public attitudes, providing leadership, education, and networks for companies seeking to join the ranks of responsible and responsive companies."

NEW MONETARY SYSTEMS
WEBSITE: HTTP://WWW.TRANSACTION.NET

Economist Bernard Lietaer has made a study of local currencies in his forthcoming book, *The Future of Money: Beyond Scarcity and Greed*.[12] Local currencies are a complementary form of money that can be created at the community level and help people move from sole dependence on jobs or welfare into chosen work and community-building exchanges of energy and talents. Bernard says that the healing of scarcity leads to the liberation of creativity. His work will help us design new monetary and economic systems to provide sustainability for humans and the environment. His prize-winning website offers the latest information for those interested in local currencies.

Network Marketing: Cooperative Entrepreneurship

Rogers Carrington wrote in a personal communication, "Many of us have spent years on our personal and spiritual development and neglected our material/financial well being. Fortunately, we are witnessing a breakthrough in a new paradigm in doing business. It is called Network Marketing, multilevel marketing, or more recently Trust Marketing. With multilevel marketing (MLM) one eliminates the middle person, advertising for business, and the need for traditional fundraising for non-profit organizations. We as individuals and organizations can take back the responsibility for providing for ourselves and for those whose programs we care about. We are becoming a community again and are taking charge of how that community supports each other in a non-competitive and productive way, where everyone wins."

Because of the harshness of our economy and widespread job insecurity, more and more people are turning to network marketing as a means of gaining independent income. Many are extremely successful — tens of thousands of people have become millionaires through network marketing in the last decade.

PATRICIA ELLSBERG
ALLIANCE FOR COOPERATIVE ECONOMICS
1678 SHATTUCK AVENUE, BOX 19
BERKELEY, CA 94709
TEL: (510) 287-8893; FAX: (510) 526-4310

Patricia Ellsberg has developed an excellent plan. She wrote in a personal letter to me, "Our vision is to generate a vast new source of funding for individuals and organizations working for social transformation. We see this goal being realized by adding an entrepreneurial element to our fundraising efforts, by intelligently and effectively participating in one of the fastest growing segments of our economy — network marketing.

"A number of us are working together to direct a portion of this dynamic element of our economy toward socially-responsible goals. If only a small fraction of people in our vast and overlapping networks were interested in participating in MLMs we could generate very significant funds for our movement and ourselves. If a portion of individuals within religious communities, the peace, environmental, social justice movements, alternative medicine, women's organizations, schools, socially-responsible finance and transformational politics collaborate in this endeavor, we can gain real economic resources to help realize our shared visions."

Rolf Österberg sums up the new business approach in his book *Corporate Renaissance: Business as an Adventure in Human Development*.[13]

Health, Relationships, Personal Growth

The field of health is expanding so rapidly that we are moving into uncharted waters. No longer do we trust western medicine alone, yet alternatives are so numerous and conflicting that it is difficult for the lay person to sort through the maze of possibilities.

THE FUTURE MEDICINE PUBLISHING
1640 TIBURON BOULEVARD, SUITE 2
TIBURON, CA 94920
TEL: (800) 249-8800

Alternative Medicine: The Definitive Guide, compiled by the Burton Goldberg Group, James Strohecker, executive editor, is the best guide I have found.[14] In it 380 leading-edge physicians explain their treatments. Deepak Chopra wrote, "This book is long overdue. Finally we have an authoritative text which will be a resource to both patients and health care providers. If you are interested in alternative medicine of any kind, and want the security of authenticity in this field, you'd better get *Alternative Medicine*."

ANDREW WEIL, M.D.
WEBSITE: HTTP://WWW.DRWEIL.COM

Andrew Weil, author of *Spontaneous Healing* and *Eight Weeks to Optimum Health,* has developed Canyon Ranch in Tucson, Arizona, which offers a full complement of medical testing services.[15] His message is that the body can heal itself. His vision is to transform medicine from something made use of on rare occasions into something that informs almost everything we do. Integrative medicine seeks alternative and conventional approaches working together, each doing what it's best at. Weil's Program in Integrative Medicine is part of the University of Arizona's College of Medicine. It sponsors formal research on the efficacy of alternative treatments, runs a clinic, designs curriculum for medical students and practicing physicians, and is instituting a fellowship program that will train doctors to spread the integrative word.

THE HEART MATH INSTITUTE
14700 WEST PARK AVENUE
BOULDER CREEK, CA 95006
TEL: (408) 338-8700; FAX: (408) 338-9861
E-MAIL: HRTMATH@NETCOM.COM
WEBSITE: HTTP://WWW.PLANETARYPUB.COM
TO ORDER BOOKS: 1-800-372-3100

The Heart Math Institute has developed a powerful and simple process to teach us to access our heart's wisdom. Called *Freeze Frame*, and developed by Doc Lew Childre, it shows us how to use a simple technique to stop stress, experience love, and receive guidance from the heart.[16] The institute has developed a large outreach program to corporations, the military, and organizations of all kinds along with sophisticated scientific research on the physical benefits of love and appreciation.

THE HENDRICKS INSTITUTE
401 EAST CARRILLO, SUITE A2
SANTA BARBARA, CA 93101
TEL: (805) 565-1870; FAX: (805) 962-0563
E-MAIL: GAYH@HENDRICKS.COM
WEBSITE: HTTP://WWW.HENDRICKS.COM

The Hendricks Institute is one of the world's cutting-edge places to evolve relationships. Over the past two decades Gay and Kathlyn Hendricks have both worked with more than 20,000 individuals and 1,500 couples in developing their method of body-centered and relationship transformation. Breathing, observation of body language, and movement continue to be mainstays of their approach to healing the split between thinking and feeling. They conduct workshops nationally and in Europe and run the Hendricks Institute for Bodymind Integration. As consultants they bring their work into corporations, churches, and organizations. Presentation material can be organized into long or short training periods. Their best known book is called *Conscious Loving: The Journey to Co-Commitment*.[17]

Science and Technology

Through conscious evolution science and technology moves toward the effort to understand the process of nature in order to coevolve with nature to realize the optimum potential of Earth life.

THE INSTITUTE FOR NOETIC SCIENCES
475 GATE FIVE ROAD, SUITE 300
SAUSALITO, CA 94965
TEL: (415) 331-5650; FAX: (415) 331-5673
WEBSITE: HTTP://WWW.NOETIC.ORG

This institute is an educational institution that attempts to apply the scientific method to the understanding of consciousness. Noetic sciences involve an interdisciplinary, experientially based inquiry into consciousness. The institute was founded by astronaut Edgar Mitchell after his spiritual and mind-expanding experience in outer space. It is the premier organization in the world that makes an understandable connection with the vast and little understood arena of consciousness and anomalies that do not fit current understanding of reality, such as UFOs and out-of body and near-death experiences. It is a membership organization with more than 50,000 members internationally, has a network of more than 300 community groups throughout the U.S. and in fifteen countries, and publishes two quarterly magazines, including the *Noetic Sciences Review* and *Connections.*

FIRST MILLENNIAL FOUNDATION
P.O. BOX 347
RIFLE, CO 81650
TEL: (970) 625-5052; FAX: (970) 625-5052
E-MAIL: TASAVAGE@ROF.NET
WEBSITE: HTTP://WWW.MILLENNIAL.ORG

One of the most interesting new pioneering efforts in outer space is the First Millennial Foundation. In 1992 author and futurist Marshall T. Savage of Rifle, Colorado, published *The Millennial Project: Colonizing the Galaxy in Eight Easy Steps.*[18] This provocative, extensive research book integrates seven proposed steps to colonize the galaxy. Arthur C. Clarke wrote of the book, "*The Millennial Project* is a book I wish I'd written: correction — it's a book I wish I could have written. I am completely awed, and I don't awe easily." Marshall is gathering techno-wizards of the future, young men and women who call themselves space colonists and actually want to colonize space. Marshall does not believe that something as important as "greening the cosmos" can be left to governments alone. He has invited me to be one of their advisors, especially in the domain of human relationships and forms of self-governance suitable to the next stage of human evolution in outer space. Marshall's foundation envisions sea colonies as a start toward colonization of the galaxy. Extensive work teams, including young people of outstanding brilliance, can participate via his website. This is an opportunity to get in at the beginning of the greatest physical adventure of the 21st century.

A FUTURIST'S PERSPECTIVE FOR SPACE
DR. KENNETH J. COX
E-MAIL: KJCOX@EMS.JSC.NASA.GOV

Dr. Kenneth J. Cox, a NASA engineer, is one of the most important space visionaries working within government. In his recent paper, "A Futurist's Perspective for Space," he lays out the evolutionary agenda for space, claiming that space is like a multifaceted diamond. He says that we must transform from "a space program to an Earth/Space program, transitioning the diversity of human experience into space and infusing space discovery, meaning, knowledge, and values into Earth/Space."

FORESIGHT INSTITUTE
BOX 61058
PALO ALTO, CA 94306
TEL: (415) 917-1122; FAX: (415) 917-1123
E-MAIL: INFORM@FORESIGHT.ORG

K. Eric Drexler, author of *Engines of Creation* and *Unbounding the Future,* is one of the originators of what may prove to be the most evolutionary technological advance of the 21st century — literally giving us the power to grow anything and everything, atom by atom, as nature does.[19] Nanotechnology is at the frontier of the infinitesimal, as noetics is at the frontier of inner space, and astronautics is at the frontier of outer space. If nanotechnology proves feasible, and many larger industrial corporations think it will, it will render obsolete much of our current industrial technologies and place the human race on the path of physical cocreation, including renewing our bodies, renewing the environment, and growing colonies in outer space. To keep up-to-date on this phenomenal new frontier, you can subscribe to the institute's *Update.*

FOUNDATION FOR THE FUTURE
123-105TH AVENUE S.E.
BELLEVUE, WA 98004
TEL: (425) 451-1333; FAX: (425) 451-1238
E-MAIL: INFO@FUTUREFOUNDATION.COM
WEBSITE: HTTP://WWW.FUTUREFOUNDATION.COM

Foundation for the Future plans to engage in a broad range of activities including the sponsorship of basic research into those social, genetic, biological, medical, psychological, physiological, cultural and environmental factors that have or will have an impact on the quality of human life during the coming millennia. Executive

Director Bob Citron, indicated that the founders intend to think ahead thousands of years. Coming from an entrepreneurial and space technological background, the founders are, as far as I know, the first to take on the great task of seeing ahead toward the next phase of human evolution in specific terms. They trace our evolution from the big bang to the distant future, asking, What is the direction of human genetic evolution? Are science and technology the demons that will destroy humanity or are they our hope for its future well-being? What are the possible scenarios for the future biological and cultural evolution of our species during coming millennia? What are our options for the future? They offer research grants, the Kistler Prize, a Humanity 3000 Symposium, and publications and educational programs.

Spirituality and Religion

In this sector we are witnessing an uprising of universal, evolutionary, cocreative spirituality triggered by the pressure of evolution, which raises consciousness and freedom at every quantum transformation. A new foundation for a universal spirituality of the 21st century is being established, one that honors all traditions, yet transcends them as we become conscious cocreators of our world.

THE ASSOCIATION FOR GLOBAL NEW THOUGHT
BARBARA BERNSTEIN, DIRECTOR
1565 MAPLE AVENUE, SUITE 204-205
EVANSTON, IL 60201
TEL: (874) 866-9525; FAX: (866) 846-9526

The association is a newly founded organization of ministers, lay people, heads of new thought organizations, social ministers (spiritually motivated social activists), and people of all faiths and backgrounds dedicated to bringing the principles and practices of conscious cocreation further into the world. It formed to bring what has worked so well for healing and personal spiritual development into the world, to heal and evolve our society as a whole. It is working toward a world that manifests the values of universal spirituality, conscious cocreation, spiritual community, self-realization, and planetary peace. It is reaching out to support all those working for the spiritual and social evolution of our world. The goal is not a new religion, but a new world.

UNITED RELIGIONS INITIATIVE
1055 TAYLOR STREET
SAN FRANCISCO, CA 94108
TEL: (415) 440-2303; FAX: (415) 440-2313
E-MAIL: OFFICE@UNITED-RELIGIONS.ORG
WEBSITE: HTTP://WWW.UNITED-RELIGIONS.ORG

Bishop Swing, Episcopal bishop of California, started the United Religions Initiative to bring all faiths into dialog to overcome the violence among religions and to establish an ongoing process of interaction comparable in importance to the United Nations. In June 1997, 200 spiritual and religious leaders met, called together by Bishop Swing. We did not meet as representatives from various faiths and traditions, but rather as individuals from every faith called to inspired action to cocreate something new. David L. Cooperrider, Ph.D., associate professor of Organizational Behavior and chairman of SIGMA Center for Global Change at Case Western Reserve University, provided the following vision for the group to deliberate on: "There needs to be, in today's complicated and interconnected world, a United Religions, which would, in spiritually appropriate ways, parallel that of the United Nations."

LIVING ESSENCE FOUNDATION
454 LAS GALINAS AVENUE #308
TERRA LINDA, CA 94903
TEL: (415) 492-1186; FAX: (415) 491-1085
E-MAIL: INFO@LIVINGESSENCE.COM
WEBSITE: HTTP://WWW.INFOASIS.COM/PEOPLE/LEF

Arjuna Nick Ardagh of the Living Essence Foundation offers a special new work: *Relaxing Into Clear Seeing*.[20] This is a practical step-by-step methodology to experience nondual consciousness, to be liberated from the fixation with the small ego Self to identify with the boundless and eternal Self. The work springs from the lineage of Ramana Maharashi in India and the Dzogchen teachings in Tibetan Buddhism, as well as from Poonjaji, Douglas Harding, Nisargadatta, and others. He wrote to me, "The main thesis of the book is that awakening is much more accessible to ordinary human beings than it has been suggested by the traditions in which such realization has usually rested. We are entering a new phase of maturity as a species in which the hierarchical guru/disciple relationship is becoming replaced by a spirit of awakening and realization in mutuality and friendship." The book gives us clear practices toward the natural state of self-realization. I highly recommend it for all cocreators.

Environment and Habitat

The goal in this sector is to understand and manage a sustainable planetary ecology to realize the evolutionary potential of Earth life, including environment restoration, species preservation, and sustainable economic development in an open Earth/Space system.

THE NATURAL STEP
4000 BRIDGEWAY, SUITE 102
SAUSALITO, CA 94965
TEL: (415) 332-9394; FAX: (415) 332-9395
WEBSITE: HTTP://WWW.EMIS.COM/TNS

Countless excellent organizations are working on all aspects of the environment. I mention only one here, for it epitomizes the approach of the social potential movement. It is called The Natural Step. Karl-Hendrick Roberts, M.D., Ph.D., one of Sweden's leading cancer researchers, wanted to go beneath the details of the debate on the state of the environment and take action based on agreed-upon facts. As reported by *In Context*, "Imagine the following: The scientists of an entire nation come to consensus on the roots of our environmental problems and the most critical avenues for action. The nation's head of state then gives his endorsement to their consensus report. An educational packet based on that report is prepared and sent to every household and school, so that citizens and students can learn the basics of sustainability. Then a roster of famous artists and celebrities goes on television to promote and celebrate the birth of this remarkable national project — a project that, in the long run, promises to completely reorganize the nation's way of life to bring it into alignment with the laws of nature."

This happened in Sweden and is now spreading to other parts of the world including the United States.

Culture, Media, Communication

This sector deals with development of cultural expression in the arts that attracts our higher nature and with media communication of the NewNews, the new story, of our visions of a positive future.

INSTITUTE OF NOETICS SCIENCES
475 GATE FIVE ROAD, SUITE 3000
SAUSALITO, CA 94965
TEL: (415) 331-5650; FAX: (415) 331-5673
WEBSITE: HTTP://WWW.NOETIC.ORG

In "The Integral Culture Survey: A Study of the Emergence of Transformational Values in America" (mentioned frequently in this
book), Paul H. Ray has described the cultural creatives this book
hopes to serve.[21] It is essential background reading for everyone in
the social potential movement.

WENDY HUNTER ROBERTS
EVOLUTION 2000
2 EMBARCADERO CENTER, SUITE 200
SAN FRANCISCO, CA 94111-3834
TEL: (415) 835-1319; E-MAIL: WHR@EVOLUTION2000.COM

In the realm of popular theater, Wendy Hunter Roberts, founder of
Evolution 2000, is about to tell the new story in a way that can reach
millions of people. She wrote in a letter describing her project, "Our
cultural binding cords have broken. The stories that have held
together our culture for thousands of years are no longer believable
to us. What will we put in its place — as the old egg shatters, how do
we replace it with a new one that binds us in sacred relationship to
the living universe? ... Why not put the sacred, miraculous story of
our own evolution, told in mythic proportions and style, in its
place? Why not ritualize the telling, combining the best in theater
and multimedia with primal ritual technique, so that it enters the

collective unconscious at a pre-cognitive level, as a telling of our own bodies' memory? This is what 'Evolution!' proposes to do. At the turn of the year 2000 'Evolution!,' a multimedia rock opera and traveling rite of passage, will begin its nation-wide, and then its international tour. It will tell our story to 6 to 10 thousand people per performance, using spectacular multimedia effects and a Greek chorus singing, rapping, dancing, and doing gymnastics. The story it tells is our bodies' story of the 15 billion-year journey to arrive here, and our imaginations' story, in which the audience will participate in creating a future of harmony, relatedness, and sustainability for all life."

THE CLUB OF BUDAPEST
H-1014 BUDAPEST
SZENTHAROMSAG TER 6, HUNGARY
TEL/FAX: (36-1) 175-1885
E-MAIL: H290LAS@ELLA2.SZTADI.HU

Professor Ervin Laszlo has formed The Club of Budapest for the purpose of helping to engender visions of a positive future to attract us forward. He has invited distinguished artists, visionaries, and spiritual leaders to come together in a variety of ways to flesh out and further communicate the vision of our evolutionary potential — to move us toward a planetary consciousness. He is setting up Centers for Planetary Consciousness throughout the world.

WORLD FUTURES: THE JOURNAL OF GENERAL EVOLUTION
URI-U. 49,1014 BUDAPEST, HUNGRY

In the field of the theoretical basis of conscious evolution, major research is underway with leadership from Professor Ervin Laszlo, former program director of the United Nations Institute for Training and Research. Laszlo was instrumental in the founding of the General Evolution Research Group, formed in 1986 to bring together a small group of scholars from a variety of disciplines and nations to explore possibilities for the development of a general (as differentiated from solely biological or paleontological) evolution theory. Its journal is *World Futures: The Journal of General Evolution.*

RIANE EISLER AND DAVID LOYE
THE CENTER FOR PARTNERSHIP STUDIES
P. O. BOX 51936,
PACIFIC GROVE, CA 93950
TEL: (408) 626-1002; FAX: (408) 626-3734

Riane Eisler, famous for her seminal works *The Chalice and the Blade* and *Sacred Pleasure,* is the first woman to be included in the core working membership of a group devoted to evolutionary research and the first to contribute an influential new theory of cultural evolution.[22] David Loye, another major figure in the evolutionary movement, wrote in a paper, "Evolutionary Action Theory: A Brief Outline," "Based on thousands of indicators both then and now, the theoretical framework that Eisler poses is that of an earlier shift from partnership toward domination now being mirrored in our time by another shift, but this time out of domination toward partnership."

David Loye, social psychologist, futurist, and systems theorist, is the author of a new theory of moral transformation. His forthcoming book, *The Evolutionary Outrider: The Impact of the Human Agent on Evolution*[23] makes the case for a new action-oriented theory of evolution that builds on Darwin's neglected but fundamental theory of the development of the "moral sense."

HUMANKIND ADVANCING
RURAL ROUTE 1
LOCKEPORT, NOVA SCOTIA BOT 1LO
CANADA
TEL: (902) 656-2085
E-MAIL: ERIER@BAR.AURACOM.COM

Erika Erdmann publishes a small but valuable compendium of evolutionary thought, *Humankind Advancing*. The aim of this periodical is the search for, and the promotion of, work that can lead our species to a higher stage of mental maturity without destroying the core and content of our humanity.

WEBSITES

Many websites are now building community around aspects of planetary transformation.

Best Practices Database http://www.bestpractices.org

Best Practices Database is a searchable database containing solutions to common urban problems facing the world's cities today. The Together Foundation and the United Nations Center for Human Settlements have spent a year compiling best practice information submitted by communities from around the world. This knowledge base plays an important role in identifying ways in which shared solutions can address urgent issues such as poverty, access to land, clean water, population, shelter, and transportation.

EnviroLink Network http://www.envirolink.org

EnviroLink Network is our largest, most frequently consulted on-line environmental information resource. As of November 1996, more than 5.2 million people per month were turning to Envi-roLink for the most comprehensive up-to-date environmental resources available.

Health World On-line http://www.healthy.net

Health World On-line is the most comprehensive natural health and wellness site on the Internet, integrating both natural and conventional health information into a synergistic whole. It helps individuals make choices for healing and opens the door to a new approach: Self Managed Care™.

Institute for Global Communications and Peace Net
http://www.igc.org/igc/index.html

Since this institute was founded in 1986 in Palo Alto, California, it has been expanding to bring Internet tools to people working on peace, justice, human rights, environmental protection, labor issues, and conflict resolution. It has grown from a tiny project to a national membership of more than 15,000, with links to networks and activists worldwide.

Right to Know Network http://www.rtk.net

This network provides free on-line access to quantitative databases and numerous text files and conferences on the environment, housing, and sustainable development that encourages citizen involvement in community and government decision making. It is jointly operated by two nonprofit organizations: OMB Watch and The Unison Institute.

New Civilization Network http://www.worldtrans.org

New Civilization Network dialogues on all aspects of building a new civilization. The network is developing 9 $^1/_2$ acres of land in

Ojai, California, and as of this writing is in conversation with a potential major donor to the effort. A New Civilization Foundation has been formed to guide this funding, if it comes through.

Global Visions http://global visions.org/cl/elkin

Global Visions is continuing to network healing, education, entertainment, and the arts.

World Peace 2000 http://www.worldpeace2000.org

World Peace 2000 was initiated by Robert Muller and is connecting many peace initiatives promoting "One Day in Peace, January 1, 2000."

Tribute 2000 http://www.tribute2000.org

Jay Gary's website keeps us informed of major developments in planning for the millennium celebrations from the Christian point of view.

Earth Concert 2000 http://www.cybernaute.com/earthconcert2000

Jean Hudon's website is a focal point for a large network of millennium projects.

Light 2000 http://www.light2000.com

Light 2000 welcomes you to celebrate the millennium countdown by joining the millennium gatherers. They have initiated the Millennium Countdown Gathering counting down 100 days at a time to the year 2000. People gather on specified days and ask one another, "What do you want to create in your life by 2000? What do you want to accomplish in the next 100 days? List three goals." It is a way of using the millennium date to help people bring their visions into action.

SOCIAL POTENTIAL PUBLICATIONS

These magazines seek positive spiritual and social innovations that build toward a positive future.

The Futurist
7910 WOODMONT AVENUE, SUITE 450
BETHESDA, MD 20814
TEL: (301) 656-8274; FAX: (301) 951-0394
E-MAIL: WFSINFO@WFS.ORG
WEBSITE: HTTP://WWW.WFS.ORG/WFS

The World Future Society publishes *The Futurist* and brings together futurists — social and political leaders from around the world — in major international assemblies each year, offering an excellent opportunity for exchange of ideas and networking. The society has chapters in many countries.

YES! A Journal of Positive Futures
P.O. BOX 10818
BAINBRIDGE ISLAND, WA 98110
TEL: (206) 842-0216; FAX: (206) 842-5208
E-MAIL: YES@FUTURENET.ORG
WEBSITE: HTTP://WWW.FUTURENET.ORG

This journal is an early tracker of the social potential movement. Editor Sarah Van Gelder states, "The purpose of Positive Futures Network, and its publication *YES!* is to show that we humans have the capacity and the opportunity to consciously choose a future that sustains and enhances life. This choice is being made every day, in large ways and small, within human communities, in our relationship to our living planet, and in our choices to become aware of, and to act on, our deepest values. *YES!* explores community, ecology, and self through stories of creative work at all levels from the personal to the global, and through tools, analysis, and information that readers can use to develop and actualize their own vision for a sustainable and creative way of life, community, and world."

Tikkun
26 FELL STREET
SAN FRANCISCO, CA 94102
TEL: (415) 575-1200; FAX: (415) 575-1434

Tikkun is a journal that Michael Lerner has created. It is part of the Foundation for Ethics and Meaning (see the Governance section).

Utne Reader
1624 HARMON PLACE, SUITE 330
MINNEAPOLIS, MN 55403-1906
TEL: (612) 338-5040
WEBSITE: HTTP://WWW.UTNE.COM/LENS

Utne Reader has been called the *Reader's Digest* of the transformation. Articles are published from many sources, focusing on the social potential movement.

RADIO AND TELEVISION

New radio and television programs are pioneering in the communication of transformational people and good news.

NEW DIMENSIONS RADIO
P.O. BOX 569
UKIAH, CA 95482
TEL: (800) 935-8273
E-MAIL: NDRADIO@IGC.ORG
WEBSITE: HTTP://WWW.NEWDIMENSIONS.ORG

Michael and Justine Toms' "New Dimensions Radio" is the premier radio outlet for the transformational movement. Michael has interviewed most of the great leaders and pioneers whose works are shaping the positive future. His programs are heard throughout the United States and his tapes can be ordered.

RADIO FOR PEACE INTERNATIONAL
P.O. BOX 88
SANTA ANA, COSTA RICA
TEL: (506) 249-1821; FAX: (506) 249-1095
E-MAIL: RFPCR@SOL.RACSA.CO.CR
WEBSITE:
HTTP://WWW.CLARK.NET/PUB/CWILKINS/RFPI/RFPI.HTML

Radio for Peace International is a short wave radio station that broadcasts globally from Costa Rica.

CONVERSATIONS WITH JEAN FERACA
WISCONSIN PUBLIC RADIO
821 UNIVERSITY AVENUE
MADISON, WI 53706
TEL: (608) 263-1233

Jean Feraca privately calls her radio program "Out There — Exploring the Human Experience." She is inspired by her sense of the collective genius of real people and told me, "The very things we hear so much decried — the breakdown of society — I find reversed in my own talk show. When you are tuned in, there is a way in which there is a magnificent flow of energy that synergizes. We are more than our parts. In my regular listening audience there are militia men, Neo-Nazis, the embittered and disenfranchised. They all find their place. They know they will be heard. I have learned that no matter how distorted the perspective, there is a truth that comes through that we need. It's like Ghandi said in his Janus perspective — "Truth is multiple and we all have a piece of it."

THE WISDOM CHANNEL
P.O. BOX 1546
BLUEFIELD, WEST VIRGINIA 24701
TEL: (304) 589-5111; FAX: (304) 589-7277
WEBSITE: HTTP://WWW.WISDOMCHANNEL.COM

The Wisdom Channel is a 24-hour-a-day life-affirming satellite program service available on audio and video, delivered currently via C-Band satellite to 4.5 million households in North America (large-dish owners). Soon 12 million cable homes and a cable channel in the Los Angeles basin will be added.

WETV
342 MACLAREN STREET
OTTAWA, ON K2P OM6 CANADA
TEL: (613) 238-4580; FAX: (613) 238-5642
E-MAIL: INFO@WETV.COM
WEBSITE: HTTP://WWW.WETV.COM

WETV delivers an underlying message about the environment and sustainable development, cultural diversity, and the empowerment of youth and women. It broadcasts via satellite to broadcast affiliates in every region of the world.

ENDNOTES

CHAPTER ONE
The Awakening of Humanity

1. Jonas Salk, *Anatomy of Reality: Merging of Intuition and Reason* (New York: Columbia University Press, 1983).
2. Eric Chaisson, *The Life Era: Cosmic Selection and Conscious Evolution* (New York: W.W. Norton and Co., 1989).
3. Eric Chaisson, "Our Cosmic Heritage," *ZYGON*, Vol. 23, no. 4, Dec. 1988.
4. Duane Elgin with Coleen LeDrew, *Global Consciousness Change: Indicators of an Emerging Paradigm*, including a Guide for Study, Dialogue, and Action (Collaborating organizations: The Fetzer Institute, The Institute of Noetic Sciences, The Brande Foundation, The California Institute of Integral Studies, The State of the World Forum. Copyright Duane Elgin, May 1997). Copies of this report may be purchased by sending a check for $7.00 payable to Millennium Project, P.O. Box 2449, San Anselmo, CA 94960. Fax: (415) 460-1797. E-mail: report@awakeningearth.org. Website: www.awakeningearth.org
5. Paul H. Ray, *The Integral Culture Survey: A Study of Transformational Values in America* (Research Report 96-A. Institute of Noetic Sciences in partnership with the Fetzer Institute. 1996).
6. Marilyn Ferguson, *The Aquarian Conspiracy: Personal and Social Transformation in Our Time* (New York: G.P. Putnam's Sons, new edition, 1987).
7. Teilhard de Chardin, *The Phenomenon of Man* (New York: Harper & Row, 1975).

8. Abraham H. Maslow, *Toward a Psychology of Being*. 2nd Edition (New York: Van Nostrand Reinhold, 1982); Abraham H. Maslow, *The Further Reaches of Human Nature* (New York: Penguin/Arkana, 1993); Victor Frankl, *Man's Search for Meaning* (New York: Washington Square Press, 1985); and Robert Assogioli, *Psychosynthesis: A Manual of Principles and Techniques* (New York: Viking Press, 1971).

CHAPTER TWO
Discovering the Importance of the New Story

1. Giovanni Pico della Mirandola, *Oration on the Dignity of Man* (New York: Bobbs-Merrill, 1940).

CHAPTER THREE
The Evolutionary Spiral

1. Barbara Marx Hubbard, *The Evolutionary Journey: A Personal Guide to a Positive Future* (Evolutionary Press, 1982). Available through the Foundation for Conscious Evolution, Box 6397, San Rafael, CA 94903-0397.
2. Stanislav Grof, *The Adventure of Self-Discovery: Dimensions of Consciousness and New Perspectives in Psychotherapy and Inner Exploration* (New York: State University of New York Press, 1988).
3. Daniel C. Matt, *God and the Big Bang: Discovering the Harmony between Science and Spirituality* (Woodstock, VT: Jewish Lights Publishing, 1996).
4. Brian Swimme and Thomas Berry, *The Universe Story: From the Primordial Flaring Forth to the Ecozoic Era* (San Francisco: HarperCollins, 1992).
5. A. Krafft Ehricke, "The Extraterrestrial Imperative," *Bulletin of the Atomic Scientists*, November 1971.
6. Riane Eisler, *The Chalice and the Blade* (San Francisco: HarperSanFrancisco, 1987).
7. Michael Grosso, *Frontiers of the Soul* (Wheaton, IL: Quest Books, 1992).
8. Gregory Stock, *Metaman: The Merging of Humans and Machines into a Global Superorganism* (New York: Simon and Schuster, 1993).
9. Duane Elgin, *Awakening Earth: Exploring the Human Dimensions of Evolution* (New York: William Morrow and Company, Inc., 1993).

CHAPTER FOUR
Our Crisis Is a Birth

1. Buckminster Fuller, *Operating Manual for Space Ship Earth* (New York: The Penguin Group, 1991).
2. Eric Chaisson, *The Life Era: Cosmic Selection and Conscious Evolution* (New York: W.W. Norton and Co., 1989).
3. John Randolph Price, *The Planetary Commission* (Published and distributed by

The Quartus Foundation for Spiritual Research, Inc., P.O. Box 26683, Austin, TX 78755).

4. Peter Russell, *The Global Brain Awakens: Our Next Evolutionary Leap* (Palo Alto, CA: Global Brain, Inc., 1995).

5. Rupert Sheldrake, *A New Science of Life: The Hypothesis of Formative Causation* (Los Angeles, CA: J.P. Tarcher, Inc., 1981).

6. Peter Russell, *The White Hole in Time: Our Future Evolution and the Meaning of Now* (San Francisco: HarperSanFrancisco, 1992).

7. Jan Smuts, *Holism and Evolution* (Westport, CT: Greenwood Press, 1973).

8. Teilhard de Chardin, *The Phenomenon of Man* (New York: HarperCollins, 1975).

9. Peter Schwartz, "The Art of the Long View," *Wired*, July 1997.

10. David B. Ellis, *Creating Our Future: A Guide to Long-Range Visioning* (P.O. Box 8396, Rapid City, SD: Breakthrough Enterprises, Inc., 1997). To order call: 1-800-335-9938.

11. Kenneth Cox, "A Futurist's Perspective for Space." May be obtained by contacting the author through his E-mail: kjcox@ems.jsc.nasa.gov.

CHAPTER FIVE
Conscious Evolution

1. Eric Chaisson, "Our Cosmic Heritage," *ZYGON*, vol. 23, no. 4, December 1988.

2. Beatrice Bruteau, "Symbiotic Cosmos," *The Roll, Newsletter of the Schola Contemplationis*, December, 1993. Can be obtained by writing to Philosopher's Exchange, 3425 Forest Lane, Pfafftown, NC 27040-9545.

3. Timothy Leary, *Info-Psychology:* (A revision of *Exo-Psychology*) *A Manual on the Use of the Human Nervous System According to the Instructions of the Manufacturers* (Las Vegas: Falcon Press, 1989).

4. Alfred Korzybski, *Science and Sanity: Introduction to Non-Aristotelian Systems and General Semantics* (Lakeville, CT: International Non-Aristotelian Library Publishing Co., 1958).

CHAPTER SIX
Exploring the Meaning of Conscious Evolution

1. Richard Elliot Friedman, *The Disappearance of God: A Divine Mystery* (New York: Little Brown and Co., 1995).

2. Theodore B. Roszak, *The Voice of the Earth* (New York: Simon & Schuster, 1992).

3. Eric Jantsch, *Design of Evolution: Self-Organization and Planning in the Life of Human Systems* (New York: George Braziller, 1975).

4. Gary Zukav, (personal correspondence).

5. Hazel Henderson, *Building a Win-Win World: Life Beyond Global Economics* (San Francisco: Barrett-Koehler Publishers, 1996); Elisabet Sahtouris, "The Biology of Globalization," *Perspectives on Business and Global Change, Ward Business Academy*, vol. II, no. 3, Sept. 1997. Can be ordered from IONS: 475 Gate Five Road, Sausalito, CA 94965. E-mail: lifeweb@igc.org.

CHAPTER SEVEN
The Fabric of Civilization

1. Howard Bloom, *The Lucifer Principle: A Scientific Expedition into the Forces of History* (New York: The Atlantic Monthly Press, 1995).
2. Daniel Jonah Goldhagen, *Hitler's Willing Executioners: Ordinary Germans and the Holocaust* (New York: Vintage Books/Random House, Inc., 1997).
3. Howard Bloom, *The Lucifer Principle: A Scientific Expedition into the Forces of History* (New York: The Atlantic Monthly Press, 1995).
4. Bishop John Shelby Spong, *Liberating the Gospels* (New York: HarperCollins, 1996).
5. Theodore B. Roszak, *The Voice of the Earth* (New York: Simon & Schuster, 1992).
6. Ken Wilber, *A Brief History of Everything* (Boston and London: Shambhala, 1996).
7. Arthur Schlesinger, *The Disuniting of America: Reflections on a Multicultural Society* (New York: Norton, 1993).
8. Paul Hawken, *The Ecology of Commerce: A Declaration of Sustainability* (New York: Harper Business, a division of HarperCollins Publishers, 1993).
9. George Soros, "The Capitalist Threat," *Atlantic Monthly*, February 1997.
10. Barbara Marx Hubbard, (personal journal, unpublished).
11. Alfred Korzybski, *Science and Sanity: Introduction to Non-Aristotelian Systems and General Semantics* (Lakeville, CT: International Non-Aristotelian Library Publishing Co., 1958).
12. David L. Cooperrider, *Appreciative Management and Leadership: The Power of Positive Thinking and Action in Organizations* (San Francisco: Jossey-Bass, 1990).

CHAPTER EIGHT
Embracing Conscious Evolution

1. Sidney Lanier, *The Sovereign Person* (personal journal, unpublished).
2. Professor A. Harris Stone, (personal correspondence).
3. Deepak Chopra, *The Seven Spiritual Laws of Success: A Practical Guide to the Fulfillment of Your Dreams* (San Rafael, CA: Amber-Allen Publishing/New World Library, 1994).

CHAPTER NINE
From the Human Potential to the Social Potential Movement

1. Dee Ward Hock, "New Rules of Business," *Fast Company*, vol. I, 1996.
2. Mary Manin Morrissey, *Building Your Field of Dreams* (New York: Bantam Books, 1996).
3. Ilya Prigogine, "A Chemist Told How Life Could Defy Physics Laws," *The New York Times*, October 12, 1997.
4. Marilyn Ferguson, *The Aquarian Conspiracy: Personal and Social Transformation in Our Time* (New York: Jeremy Tarcher/Putnam, 1987).

CHAPTER TEN
Testing the Waters

1. David L. Cooperrider, "Appreciative Inquiry: A Constructive Approach to Organizational Development and Change," *Research and Organizational Change and Development*, vol. I (Greenwich, CT: J.A.I. Press, Inc., 1987). David L. Cooperrider may be reached at the Weatherhead School of Management, Case Western Reserve University, 10900 Euclid Ave., Cleveland, OH 44106.
2. Alvin Toffler, *Future Shock* (New York: Random House, 1984); and Alvin Toffler, *The Third Wave* (New York: Bantam, 1991).

CHAPTER ELEVEN
A Spirit-Motivated Plan of Action for the 21st Century

1. David L. Cooperrider and Charleyse Pratt, "Appreciative Inquiry: A Constructive Approach to Organizational Development and Change," *Research and Organizational Change and Development*, vol. I (Greenwich, CT: J.A.I. Press, Inc., 1987).
2. Nicholas Albery, *The Book of Visions: An Encyclopedia of Social Inventions* (Virgin Books, reprinted by the Institute of Social Inventions, 1995).
3. Eleanor LeCain, *What's Working in America* (forthcoming).
4. Jay Mathews, "The Teacher Who Threw Away the Book." *Washington Post*, September 7, 1994.
5. David L. Cooperrider and Charleyse Pratt, "Appreciative Inquiry: A Constructive Approach to Organizational Development and Change," *Research and Organizational Change and Development*, vol. I (Greenwich, CT: J.A.I. Press, Inc., 1987).
6. The United Nations University's Millennium Project can be reached at: 4421 Garrison St. N.W., Washington, D.C. 20016-4055. E-mail: jglenn@igc.org. Website: http://nko.org/millennium.

7. Eleanor LeCain, (personal correspondence).

8. The Center for What Works: 1220 Broadway, Suite 704, New York, NY 10001. Tel: 1-800-34-WORKS. Website: www.whatworks.org.

9. Marianne Williamson, *A Return to Love* (New York: HarperCollins, 1996); and Marianne Williamson, *The Healing of America* (New York: Simon & Schuster, 1997). Marianne's political organization is American Renaissance Alliance: 1187 Coast Village Road, Suite 1-492, Santa Barbara, CA 93108. Tel: (805) 565-8757. Website: www.marianne.com.

10. Corinne McLaughlin and Gordon Davidson, *Spiritual Politics: Changing the World from the Inside Out* (New York: Ballantine Books, 1994). Center for Visionary Leadership: 3408 Wisconsin Ave., N.W., Suite 200, Washington, D.C. 20016.

CHAPTER TWELVE
A Pattern of Transformation Revealed

1. Mihaly Csikszentmihalyi, *The Evolving Self: A Psychology for the Third Millennium* (New York: HarperCollins, 1993).

2. Carl Jung, *Synchronicity: An Acausal Connecting Principle* (Princeton, NJ: Princeton University Press, 1969).

3. Eric Jantsch, *Design for Evolution: Self-Organization and Planning in the Life of Human Systems* (New York: George Braziller, 1975).

CHAPTER THIRTEEN
The NewNews

1. David B. Ellis and Stan Lankowitz, *Creating Your Future: A Guide to Long Range Visioning* (Rapid City, SD: Breakthrough Enterprises, 1997); and *Human Being: A Manual for Happiness, Health, Love, and Wealth* (Rapid City, SD: Breakthrough Enterprises, 1997).

2. James Redfield, *The Tenth Insight* (New York: Warner Books, Inc, 1996); and James Redfield, *The Celestine Vision* (New York: Warner Books, Inc., 1997).

CHAPTER FOURTEEN
Education for Conscious Evolution

1. Ralph Abraham, *Chaos, Gaia, Eros* (San Francisco: HarperSanFrancisco. 1994).

2. Barbara Marx Hubbard, (personal journal).

3. Gregory Bateson, *Mind and Nature, A Necessary Unity* (New York: Bantam, 1979).

4. Dana Wechsler Linden and Dyan Machar, "The Disinheritors," *Forbes*, May 1997.

5. Teilhard de Chardin, *The Future of Man* (New York: HarperCollins, 1959); Ervin Laszlo, *Evolution: The Grand Synthesis* (Boston and London: New Science Library, Shambhala, 1987); Ervin Laszlo, *The Whispering Pond: A Personal Guide to the Emerging Vision of Science* (Rockport, MA: Element, 1996): Beatrice Bruteau, *God's Ecstasy: The Creation of a Self-Creating World* (New York: Crossroad, 1997); Beatrice Bruteau, *Evolution Toward Divinity: Teilhard and the Hindu Tradition* (Wheaton, IL: The Theosophical Publishing House, 1974); Brian Swimme and Thomas Berry, *The Universe Story: From the Primordial Flaring Forth to the Ecozoic Era* (San Francisco: HarperCollins, 1992); Hazel Henderson, *Building a Win-Win World: Life Beyond Global Economics* (San Francisco: Barrett-Koehler Publishers, 1996); Hazel Henderson, *The Politics of the Solar Age: Alternatives to Economics.* (New York: Anchor Press/Doubleday, 1981); Jonas Salk, *Anatomy of Reality: Merging of Intuition and Reason* (New York: Columbia University Press, 1983); Abraham H. Maslow, *Toward a Psychology of Being*, 2nd Edition (New York: Van Nostrand Reinhold, 1982); Abraham H. Maslow, *The Further Reaches of Human Nature* (New York: Penguin/Arkana, 1993); Buckminster Fuller, *Critical Path* (New York: St. Martin's Press, 1981); Duane Elgin, *Awakening Earth: Exploring the Human Dimensions of Evolution* (New York: William Morrow and Company, Inc., 1993); Elisabet Sahtouris, *GAIA: The Human Journey from Chaos to Cosmos* (New York: Simon & Schuster, 1987); Elisabet Sahtouris, *Earth Dance: Living Systems in Evolution* (Alameda, CA: Metalog Books, 1995) Metalog Books, 124 Justin Circle, Alameda, CA 94502; Elisabet Sahtouris, with Willis Harman, *Biology Revisited* (To be published by Institute of Noetic Sciences and North Atlantic); Peter Russell, *The Global Brain Awakens: Our Next Evolutionary Leap* (Palo Alto, CA: Global Brain Inc., 1995); Peter Russell, *The White Hole in Time: Our Future Evolution and the Meaning of Now* (San Francisco: HarperSanFrancisco, 1992); Eric Chaisson, *The Life Era: Cosmic Selection and Conscious Evolution* (New York: W.W. Norton and Co., 1989); Riane Eisler, *The Chalice and the Blade* (San Francisco: HarperSanFrancisco, 1987); Ken Wilber, *Sex, Ecology, Spirituality: The Spirit of Evolution* (Boston and London: Shambhala, 1995); and Ken Wilber, *A Brief History of Everything* (Boston and London: Shambhala, 1996).

6. Michael Grosso, *The Millennium Myth: Love and Death at the End of Time* (Wheaton, IL: Quest Books, 1995).

7. Richard Maurice Bucke, M.D., *Cosmic Consciousness: A Classic Investigation of the Development of Man's Mystic Relationship to the Infinite* (New York: E.P. Dutton, 1969).

8. Fred Polak, *The Image of the Future: The 21st Century and Beyond* (Buffalo, NY: Prometheus Books, 1976).

9. O.W. Markley, "Human Consciousness in Transformation," *Evolution and Consciousness in Human Systems in Transition,* edited by Erich Jantsch and Conrad H. Waddington (Reading, MA: Addison-Wesley, 1976).

10. Hazel Henderson, *The Politics of the Solar Age* (Garden City, NY: Anchor Press/Doubleday, 1981).

11. Eric K. Drexler, *The Engines of Creation: The Coming Era of Nanotechnology* (New York: Anchor Books/Doubleday, 1986).

CHAPTER FIFTEEN
The Great Awakening

1. Ken Carey, *The Third Millennium: Living in the Posthistoric World* (San Francisco: HarperSanFrancisco, 1995).

2. Teilhard de Chardin, *The Future of Man* (New York: HarperCollins, 1959).

CHAPTER SIXTEEN
The Cocreative Society Revealed

1. Gary Zukav, *The Seat of the Soul* (New York: Simon & Schuster, 1990).

2. Ervin Laszlo, *The Whispering Pond: A Personal Guide to the Emerging Vision of Science* (Rockport, MA: Element, 1996).

3. Michael Murphy, *The Future of the Body: Explorations into the Further Evolution of Human Nature* (Los Angeles: Jeremy P. Tarcher, Inc., 1992).

4. Jerome Clayton Glenn, *Future Mind: Artificial Intelligence: Merging the Mystical and the Technological in the 21st Century* (Washington, D.C.: Acropolis Books, Ltd., 1989).

5. Deepak Chopra, *Ageless Body, Timeless Mind* (New York: Random House, 1993).

6. Eric Drexler, *Engines of Creation: The Coming Era of Nanotechnology* (New York: Anchor Books, Doubleday, 1986).

7. James Redfield, *The Tenth Insight* (New York: Warner Books, Inc., 1996); and James Redfield, *The Celestine Vision* (New York: Warner Books, Inc., 1997).

8. Barbara Marx Hubbard, *The Evolutionary Journey* (San Francisco: The Evolutionary Press, 1982). May be ordered from The Foundation for Conscious Evolution.

RESOURCES
Vital Initiatives for Conscious Evolution

1. Corinne McLaughlin and Gordon Davidson, *Spiritual Politics: Changing the World from the Inside Out* (New York: Ballantine Books, 1994).

2. Eleanor LeCain, *What's Working in America* (forthcoming).

3. Michael Lerner, *The Politics of Meaning: Restoring Hope and Possibility in an Age of Cynicism* (New York: Addison-Wesley Publishing Co., 1996).

4. Neale Donald Walsch, *Conversations with God: An Uncommon Dialogue, Book 1* (New York: G.P. Putnam's Sons, 1995); and *Book 2* (Charlottesville, VA: Hampton Roads Publishing Company, Inc., 1997).

5. Gary Zukav, *The Seat of the Soul* (New York: Simon & Schuster, 1990); and *Universal Human* (forthcoming).

6. Jean Houston, *A Passion for the Possible: A Guide to Realizing Your True Potential* (San Francisco: HarperSanFrancisco, 1997); and Jean Houston, *The Mythic Life: Learning to Live Our Greater Story* (San Francisco: HarperSanFrancisco, 1996).

7. Robert Muller, *New Genesis* (Garden City, New York: Doubleday, 1982).

8. Jacquelyn Small, *Transformers: The Therapists of the Future* (Marina del Rey, CA: DeVorss, 1982).

9. Sidney J. Parnes, *A Source Book for Creative Problem-Solving: A Fifty-Year Digest of Proven Innovation Process* (Buffalo, NY: Creative Education Foundation Press, 1992).

10. Oliver W. Markley, "The Fourth Wave — A Visionary Forecast for the Future of SpaceShip Earth." Available through http://www.cl.uh.edu/futureweb/spaceship.html.

11. David B. Ellis, *Becoming a Master Student* (Boston: Houghton Mifflin, 1986); *Creating Your Future* (Boston: Houghton Mifflin, 1996); *Human Being: A Manual for Happiness, Health, Love, and Wealth* (Rapid City, SD: Breakthrough Enterprises, 1995). To order call: 1-800-335-9938.

12. Bernard Lietaer, *The Future of Money: Beyond Scarcity and Greed* (forthcoming).

13. Rolf Österberg, *Corporate Renaissance: Business as an Adventure in Human Development* (Mill Valley, CA: Nataraj, 1993).

14. The Burton Goldberg Group, James Strohecker, Executive Editor, *Alternative Medicine: The Definitive Guide* (Puyallup, WA: Future Medicine Publishing, Inc., 1994).

15. Andrew Weil, *Spontaneous Healing* (New York: Knopf, 1995); and Andrew Weil, *Eight Weeks to Optimum Health* (New York: Knopf, 1997).

16. Doc Lew Childre, *Freeze Frame* (Boulder Creek, CA: Planetary Publishers, 1994); and Doc Lew Childre, *Self Empowerment: The Heart Approach to Stress Management* (Boulder Creek, CA: Planetary Publishers, 1994). Both books may be ordered from Planetary, P.O. Box 66, 14700 West Park Avenue, Boulder Creek, CA 95006. Tel: 1-800 372-3100; Fax: (408) 338-9861. Website: www.planetarypub.com.

17. Gay and Kathlyn Hendricks, *Conscious Loving: The Journey to Co-Commitment* (New York: Bantam, 1992).

18. Marshall T. Savage, *The Millennial Project: Colonizing the Galaxies in Eight Easy Steps* (Canada: Little Brown, 1994).

19. K. Eric Drexler, *Engines of Creation: The Coming Era of Nanotechnology* (New York: Anchor Books/Doubleday, 1986); K. Eric Drexler and Chris Peterson with Gayle Pergamit, *Unbounding the Future: The Nanotechnology Revolution* (New York: William Morrow and Company, Inc., 1991).

20. Arjuna Nick Ardagh, *Relaxing Into Clear Seeing* (Terra Linda, CA: Self X Press, 1998). To order call (415) 492-1186.

21. Paul H. Ray, "The Integral Culture Survey: A Study of the Emergence of Transformational Values in America" (Research Report 96-A. Institute of Noetic Science in partnership with the Fetzer Institute. May be ordered from the Institute).

22. Riane Eisler, *The Chalice and the Blade* (San Francisco: HarperSanFrancisco, 1987); and Riane Eisler, *Sacred Pleasure: Sex, Myth, and the Politics of the Body — New Paths to Power and Love* (San Francisco: HarperSanFrancisco, 1996).

23. David Loye, *The Evolutionary Outrider: The Impact of the Human Agent on Evolution* (forthcoming).

ABOUT THE AUTHOR

Barbara Marx Hubbard is a noted futurist, author, and public speaker. She is president of the Foundation for Conscious Evolution. One of the co-founding board members of the World Future Society, her books include: *The Hunger of Eve*, *The Evolutionary Journey*, *The Revelation*, and *Conscious Evolution*. In the 1970s she co-founded The Committee for the Future, co-designing twenty-five SYNCON (SYNergistic CONvening) conferences to find win-win solutions in light of our new potentials. She also wrote and narrated "The Theater for the Future," a multimedia story of creation with a vision of our long-range future. In the 1980s she presented a 14-part television series, Potentials, interviewing some of our greatest futurists, including Buckminster Fuller, Norman

Cousins, Gene Roddenberry, Willis Harman, and others. (This series is now available on home video.) In 1984 her name was placed in nomination for the vice presidency of the United States on the Democratic ticket. She also co-designed three major Soviet-American citizen summits during the early 1980s.

Hubbard graduated cum laude from Bryn Mawr College with a B.A. in Political Science. She also studied at L'Ecole des Sciences Politiques and the Sorbonne in Paris. She has five children and five grandchildren and lives in Northern California.

If you enjoyed *Conscious Evolution*, we highly recommend the following books and cassettes:

The Chalice & the Blade: Our History, Our Future by Riane Eisler. In this new, accessible audio adaptation of her ground-breaking classic, Eisler eloquently reconstructs a prehistoric culture based on partnership rather than domination. *The Chalice & the Blade* provides new scripts for living, proving that a better future is possible, and is in fact firmly rooted in the drama of our past. (Audio.)

Miracles of Mind: Exploring Nonlocal Consciousness and Spiritual Healing by Russell Targ and Jane Katra, Ph.D. In this inspiring investigation of the mind's power, pioneering physicist Russell Targ and spiritual healer Jane Katra explore how our mind's ability to transcend the limits of space and time is linked to our capacity for healing. (Hardcover.)

A Call for Connection: Solutions for Creating a More Compassionate World by Gail Bernice Holland. Through interviews with leaders in business, education, medicine, the arts, science, and religion, journalist Gail Holland presents a wide range of solutions to personal and societal problems. With an extensive resource guide, *A Call for Connection* is the perfect survey of "what's working" for readers to get involved. (Paperback, available Spring 1998.)

For the Love of God, edited by Richard Carlson, Ph.D. and Benjamin Shield, Ph.D. A magnificent collection of twenty-six original essays by Andrew Harvey, Riane Eisler, the Dalai Lama, Mother Teresa, David Steindl-Rast, Matthew Fox, Wayne Dyer, Shakti Gawain, and others on developing understandings of a higher power. (Hardcover and audio.)

Visionary Business by Marc Allen. This enlightened business book is an empowering and inspiring look at the possibilities of right livelihood and creative leadership, for anyone who seeks the balance between entrepreneurial success and personal fulfillment. (Paperback and audio.)

New World Library is dedicated to
publishing books and cassettes that inspire
and challenge us to improve the quality
of our lives and our world.

Our books and tapes are available
in bookstores everywhere.
For a catalog of our complete library
of fine books and cassettes, contact:

New World Library
14 Pamaron Way
Novato, CA 94949

Phone: (415) 884-2100
Fax: (415) 884-2199
Or call toll-free: (800) 972-6657
Catalog requests: Ext. 50
Ordering: Ext. 52

E-mail: escort@nwlib.com
Website: http://www.nwlib.com